ROXY DUNN

Emily Dickinson

THE MIND OF THE POET

Emily Dickinson

THE MIND OF THE POET

ALBERT J. GELPI

Harvard University Press

Cambridge, Massachusetts

1965

TO MY MOTHER

AND TO THE MEMORY OF MY FATHER

PREFACE

I think of the chapters of this book as a series of concentric circles of widening diameter around certain fixed points of reference. There are several biographies of Emily Dickinson and a growing number of textual analyses. What is needed at this point, it seems to me, is an attempt to bring the two approaches more closely together, to use the poems and letters to get beyond the biographical data to the design of the poet's mind, since, as Emerson noted, the biography of genius is internal rather than external. Despite all the activity and research Emily Dickinson remains a shadowy and inscrutable figure. The reasons for hesitating at the threshold of her sensibility are persuasive enough. Hers is a very private world: a polar place of resonating silence. She left no memoirs, no essays. Her guarded remarks about herself, about religion, metaphysics, and art are scattered in fragments which are usually indirect, often cryptic, and sometimes indecipherable. My intention has been to comprehend Emily Dickinson not as a quaint figure or as a case study or as a verbal technician, but most fully and richly as a poet; and in addition to suggest how central and radial a figure she is in the sweep of the American imagination from Jonathan Edwards to Robert Lowell, from Anne Bradstreet to Marianne Moore.

I thought it important to identify for the reader every quotation from Emily Dickinson. Poems or substantial passages from poems are identified in the text; the rest of the citations are notes. Since paragraphs weave together many phrases and references from various places, I have usually gathered the citations into a single note near or at the end of the paragraph. The references to the Johnson texts of the poems and the letters are abbreviated: the *Letters*, by L, followed by the volume and page numbers; the *Poems*, by P, with the number of the poem and the volume and page numbers. I have also used the notes to establish patterns of theme and imagery and to connect a given passage with associated passages. I have altered the punctuation and capitalization of the Johnson texts only in instances at the beginning or the end of a quotation where clarity and fluency in a sentence of mine seemed to require it.

The most important fact of my education was the opportunity to know, work under, and learn from Professor Perry Miller. Students of his will realize how much of the background and how many of the points of departure derive from his writings and from his lectures on American Romanticism. So real is my indebtedness that just a few weeks before his death I told him, in a serious jest, that he was the Oversoul of this book. Here let me salute him as a challenging and demanding teacher, as a mind whose explorations of American intellectual history have made him a figure in that history, and as a human being whose great heart was an inspiration.

I want to thank John L. Sweeney for his meticulous attention and his unfailing sensitivity to poets and poetry, which have vastly improved what I say and how I say it. To Adrienne Rich I am deeply grateful not only for giving me the poem which introduces the book but also for giving me the perfect reading, in which spontaneous empathy and intellectual rigor worked together toward a strengthening and clarification of the argument. There are other friends — Barbara Charlesworth, Joel Porte, Robert Kiely: we are too close for me to find the right words, so let me just say that their faith, interest, and suggestions were always on call and often called upon. The manuscript was completed through the generosity of the Henry P. Kendall Foundation. Those whom I have mentioned are in no way responsible for the shortcomings of the book, but they are in large part and in various ways responsible for its existence. And for that I thank them.

A.J.G.

Lowell House
November 2, 1964

CONTENTS

E.

'Halfcracked' to Higginson, living,
afterward famous in garbled versions —
your hoard of dazzling scraps a battlefield —
now your old snood

mothballed at Harvard
and you in your variorum monument
equivocal to the end —
who are you?

Gardening the day-lily,
wiping the wine-glass stems,
your thought pulsed on behind
a forehead battered paper-thin,

you, woman, masculine
in singlemindedness,
for whom the word was more
than a symptom —

a condition of being.
Till the air buzzing with spoiled language
sang in your ears
of Perjury

and in your halfcracked way you chose
silence for entertainment,
chose to have it out at last
on your own premises.

Adrienne Rich

Emily Dickinson

THE MIND OF THE POET

THE PROBLEM OF
THE ONE AND THE TWO

In June 1852 Emily Dickinson wrote a letter to Susan Gilbert, her closest friend and her brother Austin's future wife. From the intimate tone it is clear that she is sharing with Sue her most cherished thoughts. The letter is bold in statement and profound in its implications concerning Emily Dickinson's life and work. She was speaking from her heart more plainly and fully than she did almost anywhere else. What she revealed was an ambivalence which characterized not only her emotional temperament but her religious, poetic, and personal life. The key passage reads:

You and I have been strangely silent upon this subject, Susie, we have often touched upon it, and as quickly fled away, as children shut their eyes when the sun is too bright for them. I have always hoped to know if you had no dear fancy, illumining all your life, no one of whom you murmured in the faithful ear of night — and at whose side in fancy, you walked the live long day; and when you come home, Susie, we must speak of these things. How dull our lives must seem to the bride, and the plighted maiden, whose days are fed with gold, and who gathers pearls every evening; but to the *wife*, Susie, sometimes the *wife forgotten*, our lives perhaps seem dearer than all others in the world; you have seen flowers at morning, *satisfied* with the dew, and these same sweet flowers at noon with their heads bowed in anguish before the mighty sun; think you these thirsty blossoms will *now* need nought but — *dew*? No, they will cry for sunlight, and pine for the burning noon, tho' it scorches them, scathes them; they have got through with peace — they know that the man of noon, is *mightier* than the morning and their life is henceforth to him. Oh, Susie, it is dangerous, and it is all too dear, these simple trusting spirits, and the spirits mightier, which we cannot resist! It does so rend me, Susie, the thought of it when it comes, that I tremble lest at sometime I, too, am yielded up. Susie, you will forgive my amatory strain — it has been a very long one, and if this saucy page did not here bind and fetter me, I might have had no end.[1]

The progression of thought in its turns and responses divulges a great deal. First Emily asks Sue if there is not anyone who absorbs and completes her submissive life by overwhelming it. How dull, she says, is our isolate virginity to women wedded and betrothed, trembling as they are to lose themselves in their beloved; yet how inviolate must our isolation seem to the wife, either dependent on the male for fulfillment or, worse still, abandoned by the brutal master to a furious craving. It is true that when we open ourselves to mighty forces, we "have got through with peace" and repose. Still, are mere peace and repose sufficient? Should we be satisfied with the morning dew or should we yearn for the man of noon? Emily "trembles" at the thought that she too may yield herself to the dangerous exploit (actually she makes herself even more helpless by phrasing the sentence in the passive voice of "being yielded up"), and at the same time she longs to feel the scorching, crushing force. So compelling and fascinating is the stress of these tugging forces that if the length of the page did not limit her, she might prattle on forever.

The passage itself reads as though Emily realized that she had summoned up a frightening, long-submerged secret to plain view. However unconscious she may have been of the full implications of her remarks, she was revealing the dilemma that determined her response to experience on all levels. For a few moments and in her own words she is caught hesitating between the desire to be ravished and the fear of being violated, between the need for integration with something else and the assertion of self-contained individuality, between the need for union with or subservience to the not-me and the insistence upon the separate identity of the ego.

Nor was this uncertainty peculiar to Emily Dickinson; her slightly older contemporaries were mulling over this very paradox, though in more sophisticated and intellectual terms. Two years before the letter quoted above, Emerson had written in *Representative Men*: "Two cardinal facts lie forever at the base; the one and the two. — 1. Unity, or Identity; and, 2. Variety . . . Oneness and otherness. It is impossible to speak or to think without embracing both." Man's perch, then, is at the fulcrum of a precarious seesaw. In *Nature* he had begun with a similar duality: "Philosophically considered, the universe is composed of Nature and the Soul. Strictly speaking, therefore, all that is separate from us, all which Philosophy distinguishes as the NOT ME . . . must be ranked under this name, NATURE." Unity and variety are for each of us the me and the not-me. Emerson saw in the disjunction what theologians had perverted into the doctrine of the Fall. As far as Emerson was concerned, man's fall is the realization that he exists as a separate entity; man "falls" into the consciousness of self, alienated from organic unity. Consciousness whispers, "I know that the world I converse with in the city and in the farms, is not the world I *think*." Faced with such a dislocation, who can act? Can anyone bridge the gap? Yes, replies Emerson, the poet. The genius is "an organic agent"; the poet's eye "can integrate all the parts." He can synthesize the me and the not-me when "his inward and outward sense are . . . truly adjusted to each other." More explicitly, "the possibility . . . lies in the identity of the observor with the observed"; a

[handwritten margin note: man has 2 realities — his own & the worlds]

3

man "is a centre for nature running out threads of relation through everything . . ." But the process is not so easy or automatic, even for the poet. Although Emerson could depict man as "that noble endegenous plant which grows, like the palm, from within outward," at other times he sounded a very different note: "The boundaries of intercourse are invisible, but they are never crossed. There is such good will to receive, that each threatens the other; but the law of individuality collects its secret strength: you are you and I am I, and so we remain." The occurrence of the last several quotations within a very few pages of one another in the same book, *Representative Men*, underscores the interplay of tensions. No matter how much man opened himself to the universe, he soon returned to his very self. In Emerson's terms, centripetence augments centrifugence, and centrifugence augments centripetence.

Thoreau, too, spoke of man's birth as a sundering of things, as if "we had been thrust up through into nature like a wedge." The life-process was the healing of the raw wounds, the knitting of the individual to his foreign environs. This sundering is also the vital concern of Whitman's *Leaves of Grass* whose opening lines begin: "One's self I sing, a simple separate person, / Yet utter the word Democratic, the word En-Masse." The emphasis is more social and political than in the previous citations, but the problem is precisely the same: "Walt Whitman, a kosmos," in stark confrontation with the cosmos. I am "surrounded, detached," conscious from moment to moment of "always a knit of identity, always distinction." So I sing the song of myself as a "Partaker of influx and efflux." The efflux: "I celebrate myself, and sing myself . . . / For every atom belonging to me as good belongs to you"; yet always the influx too:

> And these tend inward to me, and I tend outward to them,
> And such as it is to be of these more or less I am,
> And of these one and all I weave the song of myself.

4

Whether we move centripetally or centrifugally, we also move toward the end of movement, for life is a race against death. Soon after the mind senses its alienation from the world outside, it becomes aware of flux and recognizes that its very existence — which had gone unquestioned — is the process of dying. Synthesis and dissolution run parallel courses — run, in fact, the same course. How can we live in the knowledge of death — a knowledge that invests life's business with such terrible urgency? Emerson might have been able, at least in his public pronouncements, to put aside the nagging question; but just below the surface of almost everything that Thoreau, Whitman, and Dickinson wrote is the death's head, demanding to be noticed. "I can't stay any longer in a world of death," wrote Emily in 1858,[2] although she was to battle the specter for almost thirty years more. The very structuring of *Walden* is a fierce effort to outwit winter's icy extinction, and the toll of "Death, death, death, death, death" throbs not just through "Out of the Cradle Endlessly Rocking" but through even the most ebullient poems in *Leaves of Grass.*

The first act of consciousness, therefore, is awareness of one's self in a separate but encompassing framework; and the condition of living, if one is to "live deliberately," adjusts and readjusts itself, seeking in multiplicity the unity to which one returns perhaps only in death. Poe expressed the cycle in this terse sentence from his last work, *Eureka*: "In the original unity of the first thing lies the secondary cause of all things, with the germ of their inevitable annihilation." The fascination of Emily Dickinson lies in the drama of this extraordinary consciousness which shrugged off peripheral distractions to fasten with almost exclusive intensity on first axioms and fundamental questions in a life-long, death-long struggle. The narrow circle of her consciousness contained, explicitly and implicitly, much that was convulsing and would convulse the American mind.

PRECEPTORS

SOME years after Emerson's *Representative Men*, which Emily called "a little granite book you can lean on," [1] William Austin Dickinson published his own "Representative Men." Among the biographies of worthy members of the First Church of Amherst is a sketch of his father, and a single paragraph is sufficient to indicate how different from Emerson's conception was the personal commitment exemplified in Edward Dickinson and his friends.

Edward Dickinson, proud of being of Amherst soil, of the sixth generation born within the sound of the old meeting-house bell, all earnest, God-fearing men, doing their part in their day toward the evolution of the Amherst we live in; in the front from earliest manhood, prompt with tongue, pen, time, money, for anything promising its advancement, leading every forward movement, moral or material, in parish and town; holding many positions of trust and responsibility, never doubted, the soul of integrity and honor, fearless for the right, shirking no duty, and dying at his post as representative of his district in the Massachusetts Legislature . . . [2]

Austin's tribute is not mere family pride. Edward Dickinson's long and hard-working life earned him a place of special honor. Emerson might have suspected that with him things were in the saddle, but Amherst did not and spoke volubly of his accomplishments. Active in the legal profession, in parish affairs, in local politics, in national Whig politics, in the volunteer fire brigade, in city planning, in the organization and management of the Amherst and Belchertown Railroad, in the building of the new church, in the closing of Amherst's bars, in the promotion of temperance leagues, in the denunciation of "the Women's Suffrage People" (he was disgusted with this "class of females . . . some sentimental, some belligerent, some fist shakers — some scolds"[3]) — the distinguished Treasurer of the College, state legislator, and congressman was indeed the "representative" citizen. As a public figure he worked unstintingly for responsible action and for business and civic improvement. No wonder that in a series of "Pen Portraits of the Prominent Men" of the town the *Amherst Record* hailed him as their most illustrious citizen and asserted that the Dickinson name was identified with "everything that belongs to Amherst"; or that a history of the college pointed to him as "one of the firmest pillars of society, education, order, morality, and every good cause in our community."[4] No wonder, either, that in 1862, when his daughter Emily seemed to be behaving oddly, he gave her a copy of William A. Sprague's *Letters on Practical Subjects to a Daughter*, or that some years later he summoned his pastor to determine if she was doctrinally sound. Quite easily (and unfairly) Edward Dickinson the public man might be caricatured as a Babbitt with a mind, a conscience, and good breeding.

But what was he in his personal relations? Here are his words to Emily Norcross, his prospective bride:

Let us prepare for a life of rational happiness. I do not expect or wish for a life of pleasure. May we be happy and useful and successful and each be an ornament in society and gain the respect and confidence of all with whom we may be connected.

My Dear, do you realize that you are coming to live with me? May blessings rest upon us, and make us happy — May we be virtuous, intelligent, industrious and by the exercise of every virtue, &

the cultivation of every excellence, be esteemed & respected & beloved by all — We must determine to do our duty to each other, &
to all our friends, and let others do as they may.[5]

Marriage sounds like a no-nonsense arrangement to facilitate the
performance of the duties which social virtues entail. Are we to
take such starchiness as the commendable concern expected of a
serious young suitor? Or is this serious young suitor incapable of
profound emotion? The grim tone persists even in the last letter
before the wedding: "The time is short, My Dear, and we shall
probably soon have occasion to enter upon the serious duties of
life — Are we prepared?" [6]

Reactions to such a man were predictable. His sister Catherine
said: "Edward seems very sober & says but little"; "Edward and
myself don't seem to *make up* quite." MacGregor Jenkins, the
pastor's son who lived across the street, remembered him as "a
quiet, austere man, whose thoughts were hidden beneath a
courtly manner," and whose "cane & stock" were emblems of his
character. Upon meeting him Thomas Wentworth Higginson
declared somewhat melodramatically that he was "thin dry &
speechless — I saw what [Emily's] life had been." [7]

Closer inspection, however, showed Edward Dickinson to be
more complex than Mr. Murdstone. With a little reflection Higginson judged that Emily's father "was not severe I should think
but remote," and even Jenkins noted the report of his tenderness
to those within his circle of affection. Dickinson's invitation to a
life of rational happiness elicited — strangely enough, it might
seem at first — a spontaneous reply from his fiancée; she did not
mind the painful farewells to family and friends because "my
dear it is to go and live with you . . . ." In her woman's way she
seems to have sensed that his propriety stemmed not from an in-
capacity for deep feeling but from his insecurity with it. If she
saw in his reserve fear of self-revelation and uneasiness with the
force of his love, her instinct may well have been correct, for in

his own way he did live up to his promise of "a more ardent attachment." [8] His letters during absences at the legislature display a gentle but pressing solicitude which is balanced only by a dutiful sense of his position; and for the children there are invariably warm paternal exhortations and admonitions.

In 1830, the year of Emily's birth, Dickinson wrote to his wife:

> I like travelling, but *home* has charms for me, which I do not find abroad, and I am happy to acknowledge that, whether at home or abroad, my family are the first object of my thought, & care; and the constant endeavor of myself & my best powers to render them happy, is the greatest pleasure of my life.

Again in 1838: "Home is the place for me — & the place of all others to which I am most attached. . ." His private life was a singular dedication to the construction of a shelter around himself for those he loved. Although Jenkins recalls Emily Norcross Dickinson as "a frail & somewhat wistful person a silent little figure," she was content with a life bent to her husband's needs and temper. Home became for all an irresistibly magnetic center; Emily wrote to Austin, teaching in Boston in 1851, "I would not that *foreign* places should wear the smile of home." The price of the smile, however, was rigorous obedience to the master's will. Neither daughter strayed from the household, and at Edward Dickinson's behest Austin abandoned his plan to seek his own fortune out West in Illinois and settled down with his wife in the house which his father built them just a few steps away on the family property. When death took Dickinson to what Emily called a new house without a garden, a stricken child described the void to Higginson: "Home is so far from Home, since Father died." With one blow the pivot slipped and "we were all lost." [9]

Emily's measure of her father began and ended in awe: "His Heart is pure and terrible and I think no other like it exists."

How could one approach a father as dreadful and demanding as Abraham or the prophets — as dreadful almost as Jehovah Himself? "Father is 'as he is,'" said Lavinia in deliberate parody of Jehovah's words. Emily's uneasiness resounds through the letters: "Father is so solemn"; "as you say, Austin, what father says, 'he means'"; "You know he never played"; "he frowned upon Santa Claus — and all such prowling gentlemen —" [10]

Despite his frowns, awe mingled with profound affection when she came to see, as her mother had seen, that in his way her somber father was "as gentle as he knows how." She could recall a characteristic gesture when he secretly fed the shivering birds one chilly morning: "Father went to the barn in his slippers and came back with a breakfast of grain for each, and hid himself while he scattered it, lest it embarrass them." To both father and daughter a recognition or display of feeling would be painful, but during the 1850's Emily was repeatedly touched by the unspoken pain which Austin's absence in Boston inflicted on her father:

Father is as uneasy when you are gone away as if you catch a trout, and put him in Sahara — when you *first* went away he came home very frequently — walked gravely towards the barn, and returned looking very stately — then strode away down street as if the foe was coming — *now* he is more resigned —

From a discreet distance she could observe and share the pleasure which Austin's letters afforded her father; he would read them first in his office alone, then publicly at the supper table, and afterward, having cracked some walnuts and gravely donned his spectacles, would settle down "to enjoy the evening" with his son's words.[11] Who would have thought that so mighty and remote a man could care so much? Who, then, could not love him all the more, knowing that, after all, he did love in his pure and terrible heart?

In 1858 Emily refused an invitation with this remark: "I do

not go out at all lest my father will come and miss me, or miss some little act, which I might forget, should I run away —" Looking back in 1880, she reminisced to Higginson: "When Father lived I remained with him because he would miss me —"[12] Her words here and elsewhere suggest abject devotion to her father's will. His dependence on her, she was saying, evoked a corresponding willingness to live dependent on him, so that nothing could deflect her from pursuing a course of self-less subservience.

Had she taken on her mother's role as well as name? By no means. Demanding were the claims of love — and granted at great expense. Nevertheless, her words of dedication have too much the ring of self-dramatization. Even if her father were as tyrannical as she pictured him, she herself was not pliant, nor by any means as selfless or subservient at home as she implied to outsiders. In 1851 she blurted out to Austin: "Father's real life and *mine* sometimes come into collision, but, as yet, escape unhurt." When Edward Dickinson took to "killing the horse" with a whip "because he didn't look quite 'humble' enough this morning," Emily sided vociferously with the horse and, according to Lavinia's account, screamed her protest "at the top of her voice." No one could deny that home did offer love and protection. But at what cost? If home also threatened to suffocate her most personal convictions, then she could not submit to strangulation. The individual was still responsible; love must not mean absorption or surrender. So with a rebel's resentment she signaled her resistance: "Father takes care of the doors, and mother of the windows, and Vinnie and I are secure against all outward attacks. If we can get our *hearts 'under'* I dont have much to fear — I've got all but *three* feelings down, if I can only keep them!"[13]

When Sue Gilbert Dickinson asserted herself in some unimportant matter against family pressure, Emily saluted her with applause: "Sue's outwitted them all — ha-ha! just imagine me giving three cheers for American Independence!"[14] Independence was, after all, a Dickinson — not to say a New England — trait. As Samuel Bowles noted in Edward Dickinson's obituary in the *Republican*: the "essence of his life" was "the courage of his convictions" during a time of "cowardly conformity and base compliance," and this same courage came to be Emily's inflexible rule as well. At Mount Holyoke she had to be chided for what was regarded as her proud and rebellious will, and when she returned home from school, she had learned her lesson well. In certain matters she would brook no rule or interference. She made sure that the ground she chose to stand on was firm and then stood fast. The grounds on which she staked her claims to "American Independence" were the three closest to her heart: religion, literature, and personal relationships.

Jenkins commented that in a sternly orthodox Amherst, Edward Dickinson and his wife "were entirely conventional in their attitudes toward religious questions." Bowles called Dickinson "a Puritan out of time for kinship and appreciation, but exactly in time for example and warning." But the family knew that it had not always been so. Dickinson did not formally join the church until 1850, and earlier the state of his belief had been a source of worry to his brother-in-law Joseph Sweetser and to himself. Even at the time of his conversion his pastor reportedly warned him: "You want to come to Christ as a *lawyer* — but you must come to him as a *poor sinner* — get down on your knees & let me pray for you, & then pray for yourself."[15] Although we can never know the extent to which he humbled his heart, the dramatic pledge of himself to God — carried on a card in his wallet — suggests the intense commitment of a personal covenant, however legalistic and egoistic. And, once accepted, the covenant prevailed; thenceforth his religious independence was restricted to occasional complaints to the family about the quality of the sermon.

"Father is reading the Bible — I take it for *consolation*, judging from outward things," Emily wrote. For her uncertain spirit his "firm Light" held a frightening fascination: "'I say unto you,' Father often read at Prayers, with a militant Accent that would startle one." [16] Here was, almost, the incarnation of the Messiah whom she was defying more and more in her heart. In the early fifties, as the energies of the convert put increasing pressure on her, Emily continued to resist in small but deliberate ways. She would sometimes stay home from church, and while the family fulfilled its religious duties, she would write letters with accounts of her negligence. The last thing she wanted was an open breach with the family, but if the fight was forced upon her, she could win the battle — if only by strategic retreat. Lavinia told Mrs. Todd of one Sunday when Edward Dickinson was "more than usually determined that Emily should go to church, and she was especially determined that she would not." When the argument reached an impasse, Emily suddenly disappeared, to be found only after the service — locked in the cellar bulkhead and "calmly rocking in a chair." [17]

With some accuracy Edward Dickinson placed a great deal of the blame for the unsettling of the young people's faith upon the spirit and substance of the romantic stuff that they were reading. Emily suggested that the new literature did raise problems for the orthodox temper when she addressed an arch query to Eldridge Bowdoin, her father's law partner. Mr. Bowdoin had unexpectedly spanned the gap between her father's generation and her own by lending her *Jane Eyre*, and she wanted to know: "If all these leaves [the note was pinned to a bouquet of box leaves] were altars, and on every one a prayer that Currer Bell might be saved — and you were God — would you answer it?" In her own mind there was no doubt that she would save Currer Bell, but with God the prospect was more dubious. Her reading might have been nothing more subversive than Dickens or Longfellow or the Brontës or De Quincey or Emerson, but her father knew that these books would "joggle the Mind." Since he read only the Bible and "lonely & rigorous books" (and these only on Sunday), Emily was not surprised that he should have thought Ik Marvel's *Reveries of a Bachelor* "very ridiculous" or judged "these 'modern Literati'" to be "*nothing,* compared to past generations, who flourished *when he was a boy.*" Having "made up his mind that its pretty much all *real life,*" he lived in the stodgy world of church and office, while Emily and Austin carried on a secret conspiracy in favor of poetry and the heart. So they hid a contraband copy of Longfellow's *Kavanagh* under the piano cover and books by Lydia Maria Child "in a bush by the door." Later, when Austin was writing letters from Boston, Emily could not bring herself to read to her father the lyrical nature passages which "I loved the best." [18]

All the signs indicated to Edward Dickinson that the social behavior of these young people would bear close watching too. Otherwise who knew what would happen? When Emily returned at nine o'clock from an evening of visiting, her father was waiting in "great agitation at my protracted stay — and mother and Vinnie in tears, for fear he would kill me." Friends soon felt the chilly blast, and one begged to be "secreted . . . in the entry, until he [Father] was fairly in the house, when she escaped, *unharmed.*" In delicious relief Emily recounted to Austin another evening at home during which the family group had been interrupted repeatedly by callers for Emily, while with mounting irritation her father rumbled to her "not to stand at the door." "Finally Father . . . adjourned to the kitchen fire — and Vinnie and I, and our friends enjoyed the rest of the evening" [19]; but only after they had all been made excruciatingly aware that friends and callers were intruders upon a private sanctuary.

Legends cropped up about Edward Dickinson and Emily's

callers. According to one of these, after Dickinson had angrily "taken her to task for her lack of decorum in staying out in the dark, talking to a young man at that hour," Emily abruptly announced that she would never again leave the house or go out with a man—and thus her life was set. According to another rumor, after Dickinson had forbidden further communication with George Gould, who in this version was madly in love with Emily, she arranged a clandestine tryst with him in a dark corner of the grounds, where, all arrayed in white, she put her lover aside (with appropriate dramatic gestures, no doubt) because "love was too vital a flower to be crushed so cruelly"—and thus her life was set. Then there is the report of Vinnie's solemn declaration that she and Emily had never married because they "feared displeasing father even after he was gone. I felt I had a right to freedom, but I was not strong enough to take it." [20] We need not take any of these stories literally; and Dickinson would certainly have been horrified at the intimation that he had imprisoned his children in their home. But the assumption, outside as well as within the family, was that the Dickinson circle was considered closed.

Still, despite her father's steely gaze Emily did visit and receive visitors, even "some members of another sex." [21] In fact, two members of the other sex became important allies in Emily's quiet struggle to define her identity. These young men were Benjamin F. Newton, the clerk in the law office of Dickinson and Bowdoin during the late forties, and Henry Vaughan Emmons, a student at the college during the early fifties. Through these crucial years of decision she welcomed their companionship, guidance, and encouragement to grope toward a new conception of her relationship with the world.

After a bright and bustling start Emily's year at Mount Holyoke Female Seminary had turned into a nightmare; in steady succession her friends were caught up in the religious whirlwind which swept around Mary Lyon's calm presence. Pledging themselves to Christ, they abandoned Emily to her private hell. The next year she did not return to school, but she had still to face her devils at home and try to stare them down.

Now, however, "Mr Newton was with my Father . . . in pursuing his studies, and was much in our family." The scattered remarks made by Emily disclose how determining an influence Newton had on her development. After his early death in 1853, she was driven to communicate with his pastor, and the specific lessons which she says she learned from the young law student foreshadow much of the course of her life:

> I was then but a child [actually she was almost twenty], yet I was old enough to admire the strength, and grace, of an intellect far surpassing my own, and it taught me many lessons, for which I thank it humbly, now that it is gone. Mr Newton became to me a gentle, yet grave Preceptor, teaching me what to read, what authors to admire, what was most grand or beautiful in nature, and that sublimer lesson, a faith in things unseen, and in a life again, nobler, and much more blessed —

From Benjamin Newton's superior mind and spirit she drew not the orthodox faith, but a different kind of faith in things unseen, for he "talked often of God, but I do not know certainly if he was his Father in Heaven." We can surmise the direction of his guidance when we learn that he introduced her to Emerson and gave her a cherished copy of the *Poems*. Visionary faith in Nature was, she realized through Newton, the vocation of the poet, and "My Dying Tutor told me that he would like to live till I had been a poet. . ."[22] In view of her life's work it is no wonder that she turned to Newton with such intensity that after his departure from Amherst familial concern apparently proscribed too frequent communication. The family had no real cause to worry about romance; there is nothing to suggest that their feeling for one another was other than intellectual and spiritual, or that Emily was anything but a "child" learning fast from her grave, gentle Preceptor. The romance was with his mind and soul — not with his heart.

The repeated recurrence of Emmons' name in the letters of the early fifties[23] underscores his importance as the one who, after Newton, confirmed and encouraged the new tendencies in her. After all, he was the bright young fellow who spearheaded the movement for a literary magazine at the college, who in 1853 wrote a dissertation on "Sympathy in Action," who explored the "Sources of Originality" in a Commencement Oration in 1854, and who concluded an essay in the *Amherst Collegiate Magazine* of July 1854 with these throbbing lines:

> The golden morning's open flowings,
> Did sway the trees to murmurous bowings,
> In metric chant of blessed poems.

To Emily, at twenty-four, such a young man may well have seemed exciting. She was charmed by his "beautiful writing" and his "beautiful note . . . too full of poesy"; in return she showed him a "little manuscript" of her own and sighed upon his graduation that she would "miss Emmons very much."[24] Here was a kindred spirit; yet, once again, although she did compose a valentine for him, "Emmons" never became "Henry," and the romantic biographer would be hard pressed to find anything more than the animated association of eager novices. When his career took him away from Amherst, she turned to the task of following out for herself the implications of her chosen vocation.

In this pursuit one of her principal weapons against her father's domination was a lively and deadly sense of humor. If she could maintain sufficient distance to savor the spectacle of his behavior, then she could live under his roof and not succumb. Since her self-defense was a humorous attack, she armed her letters with barbs. When "the grand Rail Road decision" was completed, she saw her father "really *sober* from excessive satisfaction." On another occasion his "mock simplicity" — with "a palm leaf hat, and his pantaloons tucked in his boots" — convinced her that "neglige" did not become "so mighty a man." She noted crisply that "Father steps like Cromwell when he gets the kindlings,"[25] and spun out the comic image of Dickinson supervising the fire brigade. Once he attended Jenny Lind's concert in Jonathan Edwards' old church, and the combination of elements resulted in a superb scene:

> Father sat all the evening looking *mad*, and *silly*, and yet so much amused that you would have *died* a laughing — when the performers bowed, he said "Good Evening Sir" — and when they retired, "very well — that will do," it wasn't *sarcasm* exactly, nor it was'nt *disdain*, it was infinitely funnier than either of those virtues, as if old Abraham had come to see the show, and thought it was all very well, but a little excess of *Monkey!* [26]

Nevertheless, all the humor at parental expense cannot conceal the respect and affection which underlie it and give it edge; nor is her ambivalence an isolated phenomenon in the Dickinson family. The entire pattern of relationships was marked by an unstable mixture of intimacy and distance, of attachment and resentment. Several times her uneasiness made Emily pose the puzzle for Austin:

> I do think it's so funny — you and father do nothing but "fisticuff" all the while you're at home, and the minute you are separated, you become such devoted friends; but this is a checkered life.
>
> I believe at this moment, Austin, that there's nobody living for whom father has such respect as for you, and yet your conduct together is quite peculiar indeed.

Stooping to kiss Edward Dickinson in the coffin, Austin reportedly said: "There, father, I never dared do that while you were living." Lavinia said that her father "never kissed us goodnight in his life — He would have died for us, but he would have died before he would have us know it!" As for Emily herself, she insisted that she would never leave her father's side because they were so close; yet she lamented that she had no parents and depicted herself as a lost child, in one poem as a little girl locked out in the shivering cold. At the same time she knew that her own temperament complicated the problem of communication; her reserve restlessly faced his: "I am not very well acquainted with father." It was a sense of her helplessness that made her delight in his enjoyment of the Whig Convention, where he was at last in his own element, among those "who sympathize with him, and know what he really is." [27] Could she herself ever come to know such a man, or could she ever open herself to him even if she did?

One of the most striking passages in all of Emily Dickinson's correspondence is the extraordinarily moving account of her last afternoon with Edward Dickinson. As a dramatic climax, it draws together with a subtlety and poignancy of nuance that is worthy of Henry James the agonizing complex of emotions which bound together these two so alike yet so at odds. No summary can convey the delicate stress and tension of her prose:

> The last Afternoon that my Father lived, though with no premonition — I preferred to be with him, and invented an absence for Mother, Vinnie being asleep. He seemed peculiarly pleased as I oftenest stayed with myself, and remarked as the Afternoon withdrew, he "would like it to not end."
>
> His pleasure almost embarrassed me and my Brother coming — I suggested they walk. Next morning I woke him for the train — and saw him no more.[28]

Here, at their last meeting, they turned toward each other, but by now the implications of even this restrained and oblique confrontation made too rude a contact. Emily averted her face lest she be overwhelmed. For her, "shame is so intrinsic in a strong affection we must all experience Adam's reticence." [29]

Once death had removed the embarrassment of his presence, Emily was free to "dream about father every night." She poured the feelings she had contained so long into letter after letter; she channeled them into a stream of elegies [30] — safely, now that love could only be elegiac and unanswered: "Home is so far from Home since my Father died."

Years before, in a fit of rage she had planned escape, had in fact put on her bonnet and fled from the house; but, "held in check" at the gate "by some invisible agent," she "returned to the house without having done any harm." [31] Why should she run away? She did not really want to escape, especially since with adroitness and spunk she could contrive to have the best of both worlds: she could stay at home amid the love and security of those whom she loved, while so managing things that she stood apart. She could even keep her distance from bothersome outsiders by saying that her father liked to have her at home — a statement that was, after all, true enough. Her purpose was to find solitude in society (a concern she shared with Emerson, Thoreau, Whitman, Hawthorne, and Melville), and if her accommodation was eccentric, it was for her successful. In a peculiar sense she did have something of both worlds. At any rate, her spirit had won its independence; she was finally answerable only to herself. The cost of victory, however, was very high.

2

Several other men must be sketched briefly into the scheme of Emily Dickinson's personal relationships. When Vinnie was pressed about Emily's detachment from people, she remarked that "Emily was always watching for the rewarding person to come"; Austin insisted further that she "reached out eagerly, fervently even, toward anyone who kindled the spark." [32] The more closely we scrutinize her associations, the more certain both the detachment and the eagerness become. Emily Dickinson did seek the rewarding person, though in a different sense from that intimated by Vinnie and Austin: the rewarding person was not the one who kindled the spark but the one who corresponded to the spark in her — or, more plainly, the one who satisfied her needs at a particular time. This is true not just of Newton and Emmons, but perhaps even more emphatically of the Reverend Charles Wadsworth of the Arch Street Presbyterian Church in Philadelphia.

Biographers cannot be sure that it was Wadsworth who provoked the rapture and anguish of the "Master" letters and of the love poems of the sixties; but from all available information, if there were a man to be designated as this beloved, Wadsworth would seem the unquestionable choice. Apparently Emily did hear him preach during her brief stay in Philadelphia during the mid-fifties. The exact date of the trip south to Washington and Philadelphia is unclear, and there is no account of a personal meeting between the two at this time. Nonetheless, the presumption of many biographers — Thomas Johnson, for example — is that the emotional crisis of the late fifties and early sixties can be traced back largely to her love for Wadsworth. At any rate, this much is certain: that Wadsworth visited Emily in Amherst in 1860, perhaps in 1861 before his departure to the West Coast, and again in 1880 (there are fragments of conversation from these visits in several letters[33]); that in the late fifties and early sixties she addressed some letters in rough draft to her "Master"; that one note from Wadsworth to Emily survives, probably from this period; that later she was sending letters to him through the Hollands; and that she spoke of him with great tenderness as "my closest earthly friend," "my Clergyman," "my Shepherd from 'Little Girl'hood [she was about twenty-four when she first saw him]." Indeed, "I cannot conjecture a world without him, so noble was he always — so fathomless — so gentle."[34]

On this basis we can speculate about the references in some

of the love poems. For example, when she wrote in 1863, "Two — were immortal twice — /The privilege of few — ," [35] was she thinking back to seeing Wadsworth in 1855 and 1860 or perhaps to his visits in 1860 and 1861? At another time she complained that "to make One's Toilette" after a loved one's death was easier than to continue living after he had been "wrenched / by Decalogues — away." [36] Wadsworth had been called to San Francisco by his religious duty, but, from the beginning, love for a man already married had been forbidden by the Commandments. Her identification of religious duty with renunciation is fulfilled in the numerous poems of the lovers' martyrdom on Calvary, and "Calvary" was indeed the name of the church to which Wadsworth had been called.

What does the identification of Wadsworth as the "Master" reveal about Emily Dickinson? To begin with, there is something strikingly disproportionate in the relationship. On the one side there are the "Master" letters and the love poems; on the other there is the one note from Wadsworth and the fact that they saw one another perhaps two — at most four — times. The answer does not lie merely in the disparity in the number of letters on each side. There were certainly more letters from Wadsworth which were destroyed at the time of the poet's death, if not before. A deeper disparity is suggested by a comparison of Emily's letters with the Wadsworth note. Here is a characteristic passage addressed to the "Master":

If it had been God's will that I might breathe where you breathed — and find the place — myself — at night — . . . To come nearer than presbyteries — and nearer than the new Coat — that the Tailor made — the prank of the Heart at play on the Heart — in holy Holiday — is forbidden me — [37]

And here are the words which the "Master" wrote to Emily: "I am distressed beyond measure at your note, received this moment, — I can only imagine the affliction which has befallen you, or is befalling you. Believe me, be what it may, you have all my sympathy, and my constant, earnest prayers." [38] We do not know which letter of Emily's brought this response from Wadsworth, surely none of the "Master" letters; but the contrast between the unabashed passion of the first passage and the pastoral solicitude of the second suggests that something is happening to Emily Dickinson that is unprovoked and unshared — something more desperate even than falling hopelessly in love with a married clergyman. The possibility that many of the "Master" drafts may never have been mailed merely emphasizes the point — namely, that Emily Dickinson, in her middle twenties and alone after Emmons' departure in 1854, seized upon a brief acquaintance with Wadsworth to distill a rarefied image for a love affair in her mind.

At first Wadsworth might seem to us an unlikely enough choice for an imaginary lover. According to Samuel Bowles, "among the 'orthodox' preachers, Rev Dr Wadsworth from Philadelphia perhaps ranks first," [39] and he was generally known for the unflinching rigor of his "old-fashioned" views. Other testimony, however, indicates that he was not all stiff backbone; in the pulpit and in his personal dealings he glowed with a "deep, earnest, simple-hearted piety." [40] A description of his pulpit manner conveys some idea of the initial impression that Emily Dickinson might have received:

The elements of his popularity are . . . a sweet touching voice, warmth of manner, and lively imagination. But Wadsworth's style . . . is vastly bolder, his fancy more vivid, and his action more violent . . . In illustrating such phrases as "Jesus wept" and "watching the dying Savior," the plaintive wail of his tremulous voice is singularly subdued and effective . . . In argumentation, Mr Wadsworth is rapid, unique and original, often startling his audience with a seeming paradox. How long his imagination will sustain such adventurous flights, and how long his feeble frame will bear such a pressure, it is impossible to conjecture. [41]

And in another account:

You feel that behind all he says there must be lying years of con-
flict and agony, of trials and sorrows . . . all this blended with deep
study and meditation . . . finds utterance through the molding control of a brilliant, original, powerful mind, of a soul whose lips have
been touched with a coal from Israel's hallowed fire . . . He preaches
consolation like a man who . . . has himself been compassed with
suffering.[42]

The girl who heard him preach might well be susceptible to his
power; although she had settled on a poet's rather than a Christian's life, she was obsessed, as the letters show, by the final consequences of her choice, especially by the prospect of death and
the afterlife. To such a person Wadsworth's combination of
secure orthodoxy and warm sympathy, of strong mind and original thought, must have seemed compelling and comforting.
Indeed, a man who combined religious faith and human love
might quiet the fears and the hunger of both heart and soul.

Besides, this man would understand her anxiety; he knew
pain through personal experience: "He would go along lonely
streets seemingly to avoid men. He chose to walk solitarily alone
along the paths of life. . ." For Emily Dickinson he was a fel-
low-sufferer who called forth and in turn needed a woman's
compassion. He was "a Dusk Gem, born of troubled waters," a
"Man of Sorrow" (like Christ the Master) who showed her his
troubled heart (like a man), murmuring with irresistible sad-
ness: "My life is full of dark secrets"; "I am liable at any
time to die." [43] When Emily saw him surrounded by a cloud of
gloom we may wonder how much of the drama was her own invention, but the important thing is that for her he was a tragic
hero.

This rehearsal of details is not an attempt to establish circumstantial evidence for a romantic liaison but rather to indicate that
Emily Dickinson was conducting an affair that could not exist

beyond the confines of her mind. She hardly knew Wadsworth, and he had a wife. But these considerations could not dampen her ardor; in fact, they suited the affair precisely. Wadsworth's physical and emotional presence was unnecessary, even distracting, to her own ecstasy and pain. He was, in an unorthodox sense, a catalytic agent; he set off the reaction but was untouched by its effervescence. Thus Emily steered clear of the hazards of contact and response; she could have a passionate love affair without having a lover. She could have the whole experience from rapture to despair, and remain as uncommitted and independent as before. Wadsworth's acceptance of the call to San Francisco symbolized the end recognized consciously or subconsciously from the beginning: she was still alone, but enriched now by the self-conceived, self-generated creation of several hundred poems about the "experience" of love.

Not even Emily Dickinson, however, could exist in a closed vacuum. In April 1862, the same month in which Wadsworth was preparing to sail, when her love affair, even though it occurred only in her mind, came to an anguished close, Emily Dickinson, by now an almost complete recluse, displayed her remarkable resourcefulness by opening a correspondence with Thomas Wentworth Higginson. Under the circumstances it must be considered a bold gesture of self-preservation. Nervously coming to the point, she asked, "But, will you be my Preceptor, Mr Higginson?" His puzzled acceptance of the role was, Emily told him later, the act that "saved my Life," [44] and gratitude chimed time and again through the letters she wrote to him until her death.

Her new preceptor was a very different man from Wadsworth, and yet, uncannily, she knew the precise requirements of her changed situation. Although the image which she associated with love and religion had "left the Land," [45] she still had her native resources; for in the single year 1862 she produced the incredible total of more than 360 poems, and Higginson — one of the most popular and influential writers of the period, a man whose name ranked in eminence with Hawthorne's [46] — was to be her link with the great world of fame and culture that lay beyond her horizon. She had been following his sweetly romantic pieces in the *Atlantic* ("April Days," "My Out-Door Study," "The Life of Birds," and "The Procession of Flowers" appeared in 1861 and 1862), and, encouraged by his "Letter to a Young Contributor," she addressed her hesitant question to him and — to her immense relief — received a reply.

The kind response came from a man whom her father and Wadsworth would not have liked, but Emily had a mind of her own. Among the liberal causes for which Higginson served as genteel champion was the new feminism, and he became a vice-president of the women's suffrage convention and a benefactor of literary females. If Emily did not care much about women's rights, she did hope that Higginson would say she was a poet.

A religious liberal besides, he had, like Emerson, resigned a Unitarian pulpit for reasons of conscience, and he listed Emerson and Margaret Fuller as the deepest influences on his thinking. He even went so far as to speak at a Boston meeting of the Free Religious Association (addressed also by Emerson, by the Unitarian O. B. Frothingham, the Quaker Lucretia Mott, and the reformer and spiritualist, Robert Dale Owen). He later served on the executive committee of the organization. His was a moistly sentimental brand of ethical Transcendentalism. He believed "in a Utopia when the world will all be united on one grand religion — caught directly from the spirit of the Almighty and loving Father." For creeds and churches Higginson would substitute "the religion of the heart": "The poorest religion that a man develops in himself, like a flower in a cottage door, is better than the best religion that was ever imported, like an artificial flower. One must live his own life and work out his own salvation." [47] Though Emily would never count on Utopia, she preferred a home-grown bloom to a hothouse flower, and self-reliance to organized salvation.

These two were an oddly matched pair. The poet in hiding must at first have been heartened and flattered by the attentions of a famous author. As for Higginson, he fancied himself in the avant-garde, for example when he asserted the artist's supreme responsibility to himself: "The writer, when he adopts a high aim, must be a law to himself, bide his time, and take the risk of discovering, at last, that his life has been a failure . . ." Emily soon learned that he could not live up to his ringing declaration, and she should have suspected as much. In the *Atlantic* piece quoted above he went on to comment crisply that Whitman had done nothing shameful in writing *Leaves of Grass,* only in not burning it afterward. Higginson's reaction to Emily's "brilliant fragments" was to inquire if she had read Whitman. High aims and artistic integrity were not shields for willful eccentricity, and in the end decorum won out over experimentation. In any case, no enthusiasm for women's rights could move him to think that women could compete with men for literary honors. Everyone knew that while they often exhibited cleverness and dash, they lacked the thoroughness and sustained skill to fashion insight into art. [48]

Emily's realization that Higginson did not comprehend her poetry in no way impaired her faith in herself; she accepted none of his literary advice, except the caution against publication. If Higginson represented the best popular judgment, what indeed was the use of publication? Nevertheless, she assiduously courted the association, maintaining the fiction of seeking the counsel of her preceptor until friendship made the fiction superfluous. Over the years, therefore, Higginson served as her principal connection with the world of letters — an essential function, since even this tenuous outlet saved the poet from total isolation. He, at least, knew, with Helen Hunt Jackson, Samuel Bowles, and Dr. Josiah Holland, that she had the dignity of a practicing poet.

Soon after the correspondence with Higginson began, Emily remarked characteristically: "The 'Hand you stretch to me in the Dark,' I put mine in, and turn away."[49] She turned away — even from her rescuer in the act of rescue; and thereafter she carefully kept the distance that separated them. She declined graciously but firmly his invitations meant to draw her out of her seclusion, and he himself saw her only twice, during brief interviews in 1870 and 1873. Emily was satisfied to communicate through letters; at this remove, she could readily understand Higginson — all she needed to understand, at least. Despite his persistent efforts and the incalculable and gallant service he rendered, he was never allowed to grasp the phenomenon which was his "half-cracked" and "eccentric poetess"[50] in Amherst.

There is a final preceptor to whom Emily Dickinson was "Scholar." Like Wadsworth and Higginson, this man was older than she; in fact, Judge Otis P. Lord had been a close friend of her father. After the death of Lord's wife in 1877 the long-standing friendship between Emily and the judge deepened into genuine and shared love. There was a release and response in this relationship such as she had never known before: "Oh, had I found it sooner! Yet Tenderness has not a Date — it comes — and overwhelms." Still, her ambivalence persists even here. She could not honestly ignore the passage of time; love came — probably could only come — too late. In 1880 she was fifty years old and Otis Lord sixty-eight, and both were assertive personalities already committed to a pattern of living. She could indulge in half-coy, half-pathetic games with Lord ("Emily 'Jumbo'! Sweetest name, but I know a sweeter — Emily Jumbo Lord"), but from surviving evidence there seems to have been no serious consideration of marriage. "I have a strong surmise that moments we have *not* known are tenderest to you," she wrote. "Of their afflicting Sweetness, you only are the judge, but the moments we had, were very good — they were quite contenting." [51] In the knowledge that what might have been was not, they must face one another with proper constraint. The withholding of herself must be a decisive element in the quality of their love:

> Dont you know that you are happiest while I withhold and not confer — dont you know that "No" is the wildest word we consign to Language? . . .
> The "Stile" is God's — My Sweet One — for your great sake — not mine — I will not let you cross — but it is all your's, and when it is right I will lift the Bars, and lay you in the Moss — You showed me the word.
> I hope it has no different guise when my fingers make it. It is Anguish I long conceal from you to let you leave me, hungry, but you ask the divine Crust and that would doom the Bread. [52]

Not only must she hold back, but, she declared with an urgency that many of Henry James' characters would have understood, the holding back is both selfless and passionate.

Although Vinnie placed two heliotropes by her sister's hand in the coffin "to take to Judge Lord" in heaven, [53] here below Emily Dickinson had only what could be encompassed by not conferring, by not permitting anyone to "lift the Bars" — in short, by the capacity of the word "No." The private and inner excitement which that "wildest word" afforded was, she insisted, more than enough; it seemed, indeed, superior to the painful risk of yielding one's self, which might mean losing one's self, to another. In her distinct relationships with each of her "preceptors" — her father, Newton, Emmons, Wadsworth, Higginson, Lord — this was, first and last, the rule inflexibly observed, so that finally the preceptors became counters, managed and fitted into the scheme of her life, while she remained vigilantly aloof. With an accurate grasp of the situation, she designated Higginson, with whom of all these men she was the least personally involved, "my safest Friend." [54]

THE MIND AGAINST ITSELF

To some the Connecticut Valley of the mid-nineteenth century must have seemed sadly retarded in its religious development. While Boston and other more sophisticated centers had already experienced the gradual emergence of Unitarianism and then the reaction from its "corpse-cold" rationalism to a radiant Transcendentalism, the most extreme movement which the Connecticut Valley could point to was a steady series of revivals in the spirit of Solomon Stoddard's "harvests" and Jonathan Edwards' "Great Awakening." These old-fashioned revivals were to flare up quite regularly in and around Amherst throughout much of Emily Dickinson's life and to possess the town for a time like a fever.

As early as 1846, when Emily was fifteen, she saw her life determined by an appalling choice between a calling of faith to membership in the church and a commitment to the world for whatever it was worth. To Abiah Root she confessed:

I was almost persuaded to be a christian. I thought I never again could be thoughtless and worldly — and I can say that I never enjoyed such perfect peace and happiness as the short time in which I felt I had found my savior . . . I feel that I shall never be happy without I love Christ.

Despite her zealous protestations, fear that her overexcited mind might be deceived into dizzy pledges kept her from attending the recent revival which had resulted in the surprising conversions of many friends. At this point her perplexity could only melt into the sentimentality which marks many of the early letters:

> Perhaps you have exchanged the fleeting pleasures of time for a crown of immortality. Perhaps the shining company above have tuned their golden harps to the song of one more redeemed sinner. I hope that at sometime the heavenly gates will be opened to receive me and The angels will consent to call me sister.[1]

Two months later she was telling Abiah that the pressure of her friends' conversions at another revival had once more brought her to the point of accepting the call; but, once again, though she felt that "the few short moments in which I loved my Savior I would not now exchange for a thousand worlds like this," still at the bidding of "the Evil one" she had returned "to the world & its pleasures." And two months after that she had concluded: "I feel that the world holds a predominant place in my affections. I do not feel that I could give up all for Christ, were I called to die." [2] Emily's world may not seem to us very worldly, but it was a choice of a temporal goal over the more elusive promise of heaven.

The year away at school dramatized further the struggle within Emily Dickinson between a yearning for the peaceful security with which Christ's love would envelop her and a wariness of relinquishing herself and the only world she knew for a promise "with a Proviso," [3] as she was later to call the Christian hope. Guided by the dynamic zeal of its founder, Mary Lyon, Mount Holyoke Female Seminary was dispatching a journal to its missionary alumnae, and during the year of Emily's residence the journal spoke grimly of large numbers of girls with "no hope" of salvation. Miss Lyon was conducting a deliberate campaign for the lost souls through a series of special talks and meetings. While she assailed the girls' consciences, her assistants scanned their faces for tears or other displays of feeling which might signal a surrender—or rather an awakening. In 1847–1848, however, there was one student particularly hopeless and particularly hard-headed about it. When Miss Lyon asked those lost girls who at least desired to become Christians to stand up, Emily Dickinson was the only one to remain seated. "They thought it queer I didn't rise—I thought a lie would be queerer." [4]

In January 1848 a cousin attending Mount Holyoke noted with chagrin Emily's continuing indifference, which seemed touched only by loss of her friends to Christ. But Mary Whitman, Miss Lyon's assistant, reported hopefully and pointedly that Emily Dickinson had attended a "very solemn meeting" on the evening of January 16 for those who "felt unusually anxious to choose the service of God that night." Emily's letter to Abiah Root the next day was urgently intent on return to "my *own* DEAR HOME" and appended this frantic postscript: "There is a great deal of religious interest here and many are flocking to the ark of safety. I have not yet given up to the claims of Christ, but trust I am not entirely thoughtless on so important & serious a subject." After the winter recess from January 17 (the day after the solemn meeting) through February 4 the Mount Holyoke Journal noted that at a meeting for the hopefuls "one was not there who had been before" and that the absentee had not even written a note of explanation. This recalcitrant girl may not have been Emily Dickinson, but there is no indication that she attended any more of Miss Lyon's sessions. Perhaps she had come to some firm decision during the vacation in Amherst; at any rate, by May, ready to return home and not come back, she was shaken but still firmly seated, stammering how hard it was "to give up the world." [5]

Henceforth, her attitude was envy of the serene tranquillity of believers, and suspicion that, like Swift's happy people, they were simply well deceived. Her mother had made a profession of faith in 1831; her father, Vinnie, and Sue became church members during the "harvest" of 1850; and Austin, last of all in 1856. While each member of her family joined the fold properly, Emily remained throughout "one of the lingering *bad* ones" who "slink away and are sorrowful — not at their wicked lives — but at this strange time, great change . . . so do *I* slink away . . . and do work without knowing why — not surely for this brief world, and more sure that it is not for Heaven . . ." [6]

Here, then, the problem lay: how to live when one could not accept Christ's call. Even if one renounced a heavenly goal that gave direction to this transitory world, one could not resign one's self to a merely physical existence in a world of death; one would have to find something which was neither the life of matter nor the life of heaven but partook of both. Where could such a mode of experience be found? It would be a difficult search and a dangerous exploit, but it was either the quest — with or without a certain goal — or despair. Perhaps Abiah was right to choose Christ and nip fancies that might prove vain or bitter in the testing. "The shore is safer, Abiah, but I love to buffet the sea — I can count the bitter wrecks here in these pleasant waters, and hear the murmuring winds, but oh, I love the danger!" So saying, she headed alone into uncharted waters — not unlike Taji at the end of Melville's *Mardi*. The reference to Taji, with his violent obsession to push beyond the limits, may appear ludicrous when associated with a life which seemed ruffled by deeds no more daring than omitting church services. But the allusion must be allowed to stand. When Emily Dickinson pushed off from the Lee Shore, she allied herself with Ishmael and Ahab and Bulkington in the dangerous life of adventurous exploration. Impelled by "the fascination of our predicament," she pursued the homeless course of the spiritual renegade without leaving

the haven of her father's roof. During her last summer, at the
end of the invisible voyage, she wrote to Mrs. Todd: "I am glad
you cherish the Sea. We correspond, though I never met him." [7]

The adventure was a gamble, she never doubted, and gam-
bling, she was told, was a sin; however, with open eyes and a
steady nerve gamblers "toss their dice again," betting on all or
nothing.

> Soul, take thy risk,
> With Death to be
> Were better than be not
> With thee   (P 1151, II.806)

Emerson agreed that the poet's hazardous task was to set out ever
"*from* the land": "Right out to sea his courses stand, / New
worlds to find in pinnace frail." But though she could claim that
"the Risks of Immortality are perhaps its' charm," she would at
other times cry out in panic, "I am so far from Land." [8] The
risks were life-long and eternity-long, and throughout the poetry
her fears recur in metaphors of sea voyages, drowning, shipwreck,
and safe harbors. [9]

How is one to confront those "great questions" whose answers
"would be events"? [10]

> To lose one's faith — surpass
> The loss of an Estate —
> Because Estates can be
> Replenished — faith cannot —   (P 377, I.299)

The cruel paradox is that men were beginning to find the microscope a better lens for vision than faith, and yet without faith
"Being's — Beggary." "Speculate with all our might, we cannot
ascertain," and yet the possibilities lurking in the grave spoil any
reconciliation to a merely natural existence: "That *Bareheaded
life* — under the grass — worries one like a Wasp"; "Dying is a
wild Night and a new Road." [11]

We are lost in life as in death. In one poem the sun and the robins' songs insult the dead and mock those who are dying. In another poem, she gropes for "My Duplicate," someone as forlorn and baffled as she, only to discover that the walls of other men's minds are "Impregnable to inquest." At such times Nature, too, seems "too young to feel, or many years too old," as if it, like God and man, "did not care." Another poem calls Nature (in the familiar Melvillean terms) a "stranger," a "mystery," an "abyss," a "floorless" sea, a fathomless well. An "Approving God" fixed for Nature an inexorable course in which each "happy Flower" falls victim to chilling frost.[12]

Man's plight could be summed up succinctly: abandonment and death.

> Without a smile — Without a Throe
> A Summer's soft Assemblies go
> To their entrancing end
> Unknown — for all the times we met —
> Estranged, however intimate —
> What a dissembling Friend —   (P 1330, III.919)

Her phrases — "soft Assemblies," "entrancing," "all the times we met," and "intimate" — suggest the blandishments we undeniably find in our world; even the autumnal end of things is "entrancing." But "end," "Unknown," and "Estranged" cut through the beguiling surface to disclose an abiding alienation, and the final line dramatically summarizes the whole poem in the concise paradox of a world in which intimacy, however charming, is the fraudulent ruse of a "dissembling Friend."

In speaking of our birth as the thrusting of a stranger into a foreign universe, Thoreau wrote that experience showed, as scars disappeared, that in a deeper sense "nature is one and continuous everywhere." Emily Dickinson could not be so sure and though she was not always paralyzed by doubt, she was at times as lonely as Hawthorne's Goodman Brown in the heart's dark forest, as baffled as Melville by the whale's riddling blankness, as numb as Poe's Pym before the apocalyptic white cataract. Some of Thomas Hardy's characters concluded that it would have been better not to have been born, and Emily Dickinson knew what they meant:

> 'Twere better Charity
> To leave me in the Atom's Tomb —
> Merry, and Nought, and gay, and numb —
> Than this smart Misery.   (P 376, I.299)

The specter of extinction, which was the primal fear, could seem at times the only grace and final deliverance:

> Many Things — are fruitless —
> 'Tis a Baffling Earth —
> But there is no Gratitude
> Like the Grace — of Death —
>   (P 614, II.472)

No pessimist knew the power of blackness more deeply than Emily Dickinson.

In this quandary, why not turn to God, even if not to Christ and His church? Emily Dickinson never doubted the existence of the Deity: "God cannot discontinue himself. This appalling trust is at times all that remains"; but the furthest extent of her faith was the plea of the good-bad little girl to her incomprensible parent:

> I hope the Father in the skies
> Will lift his little girl —
> Old fashioned — naughty — everything —
> Over the stile of "Pearl".   (P 70, I.56)

She could speak even more casually, calling Him "Our Old Neighbor — God" and acting the child too self-consciously to conceal the desperation under her coyness:

Papa above!
Regard a Mouse
O'erpowered by the Cat!
Reserve within thy kingdom
A "Mansion" for the Rat!   (P 61, I.46)

She pleaded as a helpless mouse, knowing well that to Him she might seem a "Rat." Her plea was desperate because most of the time the "Old Neighbor" had receded "more than a firmament —from Me—" beyond the moon and stars. In His remote seat He seemed a Father to others but not to her—parentless in heaven as she sometimes seemed on earth. She "prayed at first, a little Girl . . . / But stopped" at the realization of how small and silly we must look to the Deity, if He sees us at all. In reverse perspective, from the apertures of our mouseholes we can only glimpse a lonesome God in a cold heaven above a world whose machinery grinds out "His Perturbless Plan." Confronted with the question why she did not turn to God, Emily Dickinson would have flashed back: "Of course—I prayed—/ And did God care?" He is "a God of Flint"; He is Jove; He is Jehovah (as He is called over and over in the poems and letters), and the Trinity is the Jehovahs.[13]

Emily Dickinson could not readily alleviate the torment, as some others did, by shedding the God of the Old Testament and Calvinist Christianity—this last remnant of the old faith—and establishing a new God. Thoreau confidently asserted that "Jehovah . . . is more absolute and unapproachable, but hardly more divine, than Jove." Emerson and Thoreau passed by the absolute Jehovah in the celebration of the earthly divinity of Pan. But Emily Dickinson felt the power of Jehovah too forcefully to evade the fact of His supremacy, no matter how awesome a fact it might be; nor could she doubt Jehovah's fatherhood, however inexplicable that might be. Much of her difficulty with both the old religion and the new is epitomized in the fact that she cried out, as neither Calvinists nor Unitarians nor Transcendentalists would, to One whom she recognized as "Jupiter my father!" and "Burglar! Banker—Father!" [14]

God was, in some ineffable way, her Father, and yet she could perceive only a "Vastness" that is "the Shadow of the Brain which casts it"—the same shadowy vastness which haunted men as different as Pascal and Melville. Like Ahab before the featureless whale, she flung a question at the mask: "Infinitude— Had'st Thou no Face / That I might look on Thee?" Although she had not read *Pierre*, she would have known what Melville meant when he wrote:

All profound things, and emotions of things, are preceded and attended by Silence . . . Silence is the general consecration of the universe. Silence is the invisible laying on of the Divine Pontiff's hands upon the world . . . Silence is the only Voice of our God.

In the same spirit Emily wrote: "I know that He exists./ Somewhere in Silence." It seemed to her (more so than to Melville) that at times "the Silence condescended" to strike her with a baffling reply, but too often He, "like the Dumb," would not "Reveal by sign—a syllable": [15]

> Silence is all we dread.
> There's Ransom in a Voice—
> But Silence is Infinity.
> Himself have not a face. (P 1251, III.868)*

Then was the Jehovah, the speechless Mover, not perhaps something more positively sinister and malicious? Were His ways perhaps not just inscrutable but perverse? Surely He seemed the strong-armed bully when He

> On Moses—seemed to fasten
> With tantalizing Play
> As Boy—should deal with lesser Boy—
> To prove ability. (P 597, II.458)

* Reprinted by permission of Houghton Mifflin Co. from *Emily Dickinson Face to Face* by Martha Dickinson Bianchi (Boston, 1932).

Elsewhere He is a ravenous "Mastiff," an "Inquisitor," a swin-
dler of children like herself. These were heinous blasphemies for
a New England woman of orthodox upbringing but, with Ahab,
she could be "Cynic" enough to ponder God's guilt.[16] His games
of hide-and-seek might entertain Him, but suppose that His
jokes should torture us to death?

> But — should the play
> Prove piercing earnest —
> Should the glee — glaze —
> In Death's — stiff — stare —
>
> Would not the fun
> Look too expensive!
> Would not the jest —
> Have crawled too far!   (P 338, I.270)

Papa above would have become the cat that torments the helpless
mouse and trapped rat. Was so devastating a vision only man's
futile attempt to judge divinity by the formulae of human justice? Or was it a realistic assessment of the human condition?

The Puritan forebears of New England were able to accept
God's inscrutability and man's isolation in a fallen world as part
of a total view of things which embraced the possibility of grace
and salvation. Jonathan Edwards expressed this acceptance more
forcefully than anyone else by understating the passion of his
soul's conviction:

> God's absolute sovereignty and justice . . . is what my mind
> seems to rest assured of, as much as of anything I see with my
> eyes . . . But I have often, since that first conviction, had quite an-
> other kind of sense of God's sovereignty than I had then. I have often
> since had not only a conviction, but a delightful conviction. The
> doctrine has very often appeared exceeding pleasant, bright, and
> sweet. Absolute sovereignty is what I love to ascribe to God.[17]

Edwards' resolution was unacceptable to Emily Dickinson. In the
full fury of puny humanity she would not succumb — and in

poem after poem she struck out (one again thinks of Ahab) at the Face that God showed. He was "that Bold Person" — "a jealous God" who "was penurious with me, which makes me shrewd with Him." The "King . . . does not speak" to her. Sometimes in dreams she "peeps" into His world; but when even this glimpse is denied her,

> . . . I omit to pray
> 'Father, thy will be done' today
> For my will goes the other way,
> And it were perjury! (P 103, I.79)

In a different sort of understatement from Edwards', she framed her defiance in a flippant act and slangy language:

> So I pull my Stockings off
> Wading in the Water
> For the Disobedience' Sake
> Boy that lived for "Ought to"
>
> Went to Heaven perhaps at Death
> And perhaps he did'nt
> Moses was'nt fairly used —
> Ananias was'nt — (P 1201, III.835)

In one poem she challenged Jove to settle their quarrel legally in the court of Justice. In another poem she saw herself in Jacob, "the bewildered Gymnast" who "worsted God" and subdued the Angel, and in three letters she made further allusions to this episode from *Genesis*, which for her was one of the most satisfying passages in the Bible.[18]

In these moments of rebellion Emily Dickinson's spirit was, in its feminine way, distinctly and passionately Byronic. The Dickinson library included sets of Byron,* and although many of the religious elders were alarmed, the Byronic vogue in Amer-

* There was an 1830 edition of the *Letters and Journals* of Byron, with notes by that other scandalous fellow, Thomas Moore, and there were two sets of Byron's *Works*, dated 1821 and 1854. In 1859 Sue Dickinson presented Emily with a copy of Trelawney's *Last Days of Byron and Shelley*.

ican literary circles touched such unlikely people as Hawthorne and Harriet Beecher Stowe as well as Emily Dickinson. Any attempt to associate the man who was the scandal of Europe with the lady who was the recluse of Amherst may at first seem forced; the notorious Margaret Fuller[19] is perhaps a more likely candidate for the role of tragic genius. There was, nonetheless, with certain necessary qualifications, a genuine affinity of spirit and feeling between Emily Dickinson and Lord Byron, as her sympathetic allusions to his romantic "genius" indicate (see L II 369, 374, 393, 433; L III 903). Although Emily Dickinson's defiance did not vent itself in movement across the face of a continent, it was nonetheless real. Her character and situation denied her even the temporary release of action or eruption. Byron's swashbuckling violence destroyed others as well as himself as he slashed his way to the foreseen doom, but Emily Dickinson's was "The Mutineer / Whose title is 'the Soul.'"[20] On these terms the rebel could seethe with conspiracy and not ripple the visible surface of her life; it was safer that way, and the only person she could destroy was herself. In both Byron and Dickinson, however, the mutiny was the Calvinist mind turning against itself and its Maker—a rebellion that is seldom wholehearted, and hence, with an adversary within and One without, a struggle that can hardly end in victory.

Like Byron, Emily "was very early a rebel" (as a reader of some now-missing letters of the 1840's said of her), and the authorities at Mount Holyoke tried without success to curb the proud and rebellious will. As with Byron, too, her combativeness cast her in the role of the devil; she told Abiah: "I have come from '*to* and *fro*, and walking up, and down' the same place that Satan hailed from, when God asked him where he'd been . . ." Neither she nor Byron could escape the sense that the thrust of the will, however magnificent, was not only foolhardy but demonic, that its drive was an impulse from hell. Her early letters are haunted by the serpent's power; she knew that she was doing the bidding of "the Evil one." By 1854 she could tell Sue that if Christ did not claim her, "there is a darker spirit, will not disown it's child." The phrasing recalls Emerson's famous aphorism in "Self-Reliance": "If I am the Devil's child, I will live then from the Devil"; but in Emily Dickinson we sense a more penetrating grasp of the implications of her choice. Although she tried to smooth her fears over ("The big serpent bites the deepest, and we get so accustomed to it's bite that we dont mind about them"), they were ineradicable.[21] A sermon on damnation, punctuated by knowing glances from her father and sister, could profoundly shake her (see L I 309), and in several poems (see numbers 986, 1670, and 1170) she associated the snake with satanic qualities: power, treason, guile, the ability to strike with icy terror.

In Emily Dickinson's closed world there was something of the unsatisfied, unsatisfiable restlessness that drove Byron from place to place. It was the awareness of human aspirations and limitations at cross-purposes, the uneasy yearning that "what we Could — were what we would" and, contrariwise, that what we would were what we could. "What we would" was nothing more or less than to answer all the great questions, to see and know all; "what we Could" as mortals see and know was something else again. With Prometheus and Faust as prototypes, Byron's Manfred stood on the crags of the Jungfrau with an eagle soaring overhead, and in the knowledge of defeat roared his grievance to the skies:

> How beautiful is all this visible world!
> How glorious in its action and itself!
> But we, who name ourselves its sovereigns, we,
> Half dust, half deity, alike unfit
> To sink or soar, with our mixed essence make
> A conflict of its elements. . .

Echoing Manfred's "half dust, half deity," Emily Dickinson called man's mixed essence "consciousness and clay" and reiterated — though less flamboyantly — the proud claims of the over-reacher: [22]

> Finite —to fail, but infinite to Venture —
> For the one ship that struts the shore
> Many's the gallant — overwhelmed Creature
> Nodding in Navies nevermore —   (P 847, II.638)

At the same time that it dooms him, the titanic greatness of the overreacher also sets him apart from his fellow men — a tragically nobler being, an outcast, and a voluntary exile. In a world of strangers, Emily's assertion that "the world is not acquainted with us, because we are not acquainted with her" parallels Childe Harold's "I have not loved the World, nor the World me." Manfred scornfully tells the happy chamois hunter to preach humility and patience to "mortals of a dust like thine, — / I am not of thine order." And in her more modest way, with little of Byron's arrogance and self-pity, Emily Dickinson also knew that special powers impose terrible burdens. It was George Eliot's greatness that denied her the "gift of faith" and made her life a struggle; and so it was with herself.[23]

If there are analogies between Byron and Dickinson as poets seeing and feeling, there are none between them as poets writing. The qualities of Emily's verse are the antithesis of Byron's expansive and highly colored rhetoric. She could compress the panoramic saga of a Byronic hero (her mask here for Dickinson the poet) into two tight quatrains:

> He outstripped Time with but a Bout,
> He outstripped Stars and Sun
> And then, unjaded, challenged God
> In presence of the Throne.

> And He and He in mighty List
> Unto this present, run,
> The larger Glory for the less
> A just sufficient Ring.   (P 865, II.646)

She could concentrate Manfred's protest in a poem which suggests not so much Byron as Hardy in the terse phrasing of its
complex ironies:

> "Heavenly Father" — take to thee
> The supreme iniquity
> Fashioned by thy candid Hand
> In a moment contraband —
> Though to trust us — seem to us
> More respectful — "We are Dust" —
> We apologize to Thee
> For thine own Duplicity —
>
> (P 1461, III.1009–10) *

How is God devious, she asks. He claimed to be our "Heavenly
Father" (the quotation marks give the term satirical emphasis)
but He created not innocent but blighted children, not so much
in candor as in hypocrisy. We desire His trust and respect but
must admit that "we are Dust." Still, that last admission of mortality can be turned into a bold assertion. In a final, flaunting
insult man proves his claim to dignity by rising to apologize to
God for His own duplicity. Nevertheless, even defiance offered
no solution and no respite, as Satan and Byron and Ahab well
knew. Emily Dickinson wrote in another poem (P 914, II.670)
that if one could not be ashamed before an unknown God, one
could not be boastful either.

This prolonged discussion of the similarities between Dickinson and Byron, or earlier, between Dickinson and Melville, is
not an effort to claim imitation or direct influence but rather to
associate an aspect of Emily Dickinson's mind with a phase of
the Romantic movement which Byron and Melville embodied so
dramatically. It is dangerous to make too facile and too rigid a
distinction between "bright" and "dark" Romanticism, but a

---

* Copyright 1914, 1942 by Martha Dickinson Bianchi. From *The Poems
of Emily Dickinson*, ed. Thomas H. Johnson (Cambridge: Harvard University Press, 1955), by permission of Little, Brown and Co.

broad distinction in assumption, tone, and conclusion is useful and valid. What associates writers as various as Wordsworth, Scott, Bryant, and the Transcendentalists is the glowing assertion that man can comprehend himself and the cosmos through the correspondence between his soul, instinct with sublime faculties, and a divinely beneficent Nature. When writers like Byron, Goethe, Richter, Melville, and Poe found no correspondence with Nature, they turned in upon themselves — uncertain of their end but relying on their own special powers.* They explored the intricate mazes of consciousness — balking at its limitations, stretching its aspirations, and demanding finally that all things, whether man or Nature or God, be proved or disproved within the individual.

Emily Dickinson was struck to the quick by that dilemma which constrains the individual not to open out but to close in, not to lose but to assert himself. The dark side of the Romantic genius moved her to insist that *she* must answer the riddles for herself or they would not be answered at all; she thrust her individual integrity against destiny even to the extremity of doom. She was to feel frequently the revivifying energies of more healthful Romantic forces, but they would not heal permanently her bruised, proud spirit.

2

The "Calvinist" mind could not vanquish its rebellious adversary because the adversary was itself, but it could press the fight against the visible church. In Emily Dickinson's case this rejection, despite occasional attendance at services and her friendships with local clergymen, was virtually complete. The irony which marks the comments on her professing neighbors indicates the

* Besides the works of Byron, the Dickinson library contained some samples of German Romanticism: Goethe, Carlyle, Richter's *Titan* and *Levana*, Eliza Buckminster Lee's *Life of Jean Paul Richter*.

distance which separated her from the "visible saints." In the same passage in which she noted the names of Theodore Parker and the English Tractarian Edward Pusey, those religious extremists on either side of righteousness, she fixed the solidly bourgeois character of Amherst Congregationalism in a concise image: "I wish the 'faith of the fathers' did not wear brogans, and carry blue umbrellas. . ." [24] The same quiet scorn pervades her sketch of the conventional Amherst lady:

> What Soft — Cherubic Creatures —
> These Gentlewomen are —
> One would as soon assault a Plush —
> Or violate a Star —
>
> Such Dimity Convictions —
> A Horror so refined
> Of freckled Human Nature —
> Of Deity — ashamed —
>
> It's such a common — Glory —
> A Fisherman's — Degree —
> Redemption — Brittle Lady —
> Be so — ashamed of Thee —   (P 401, I.314)

All smug and priggish, these Victorian gentlewomen are symbolized in the overstuffed and sterile inviolability of their plush-and-dimity parlors. But as the poem examines their inviolability, spinelessness hardens into haughty superiority and finally into a cold brittleness which the rough hand of Judgment will shatter. The unspoken assumption of the irony is the poet's refusal to shrink from contact with this freckled world.

In the men who set the public tone of the thriving community, the legalistic categories of the federal theology had long since become absorbed into the business mentality of profit and loss, stocks and bonds. So, individual conscience had become confused with laissez faire; the covenant, with the contract:

46

You're right — "the way *is* narrow" —
And "difficult the Gate" —
And "few there be" — Correct again —
That "enter in — thereat" —

'*Tis* Costly — So are *purples*!
'Tis just the price of *Breath* —
With but the "Discount" of the *Grave* —
Termed by the *Brokers* — "*Death*"!

And after *that* — there's Heaven —
The *Good* Man's — "*Dividend*" —
And *Bad* Men — "go to Jail" —
I guess — (P 234, I.169)

The quotation marks and italics wryly imply how little the poet's neighbors comprehended the difficulty and narrowness of the way. So difficult is the course of human life that in the last stanza she questions whether men can be sorted into theological categories — good and bad, saved and lost — as readily as the church suggests.

In 1873 she commented coolly: "There is what is called an 'awakening' in the church . . ." The "awakening" she had experienced had made her heart withdraw from a "Heavenly Clause" full of loopholes: one which promised delivery of goods, purchased sight unseen, at an unspecified future date — and then only on the fulfillment of certain stringent conditions by the purchaser: [25]

They speak of what we owe —
But that negotiation
I'm not a Party to — (P 1270, III.884)

Neither cutting irony nor broad condemnation, however, gives the sense of her mind as plainly as her comments on specific matters of Christian belief.[26] Taken together, these amount to an emphatic NO, registered not in Melville's thunder but with a crisp feminine clarity. First of all, her remarks about Scripture indicate that she was aware — in general terms, if not in argumentative detail — of the questions raised by Darwinism and the Higher Criticism.[27] "The Fiction of 'Santa Claus'," she remarked, "always reminds me of the reply to my early question of 'Who made the Bible' — 'Holy Men moved by the Holy Ghost,' and though I have now ceased my investigations, the Solution is insufficient." Her remarks fall into a pattern: "Austin told me confidentially 'there is no such person as Elijah'"; Eden is "a legend — dimly told — / Eve — and the Anguish — Grandame's story —"; "Ararat's a Legend — now — / And no one credits Noah — "; " 'I have finished,' said Paul, 'the faith.' * We rejoice that he did not say discarded it." The consistent implication is that the Bible must be considered as a humanly, not a divinely, inspired document, as a "romance" or "myth." [28]

If the New Testament is myth, then Jesus is not God but man, just as Emerson had heretically proclaimed. For both poets Jesus was the representative man: for Emerson, the man-god; for Emily, the suffering man, the Man of Sorrows (as she also called the Reverend Wadsworth). "When Jesus tells us about his Father," Emily wrote, "we distrust him. When he shows us his Home, we turn away, but when he confides to us that he is 'acquainted with Grief,' we listen, for that also is an Acquaintance of our own." She did not know His Father; pain and disillusionment were their only mutual friends. "The loveliest sermon I ever heard was the disappointment of Jesus in Judas. It was told like a mortal story of intimate young men." [29]

In a letter written during the last year of her life, Emily adapted a phrase from Scripture to her own purpose and asked if the recipient had ever thought that the words had "other than a theological import." For Emily Dickinson they certainly did;

---

* Actually St. Paul wrote (II Tim 4:7): "I have finished my course, I have kept the faith," and Emily's paraphrase changes the meaning.

they were the literary expression of human situations and human truths, and she resorted to Biblical allusion throughout the poetry and the letters. So irreverently could she take the words of Holy Scripture that her sharp wit regularly turned them to her own humorous ends. In the attempt to make Emily a good Christian despite her eccentricities, some biographers berate the humorless critic who would take her little jokes at face value as intentional irreverence. A person may joke about something sacred because he takes it seriously in its sacred context, but then the humor depends upon belief for its effect. With Emily Dickinson, the question is whether she was doing this, or whether she was manipulating Biblical passages often for the literary effect of outlandish ornament or impious humor. Especially startling are the occasions when she appropriated Christ's words to herself or applied them to others.[30] She parodied the Lord's Prayer; told Abiah Root " 'yet a little while I am with you, and again a little while and I am *not* with you' because you go to your mother"; sent word to Mrs. Holland's new grandson that "the Little Boy in the Trinity had no Grandmama, only a Holy Ghost"; and spoke to Sue of " 'thy Son — Our' Nephew." She likened a crow in a tree to Christ on the cross and then cooed, "Could you condone the profanity?" Punning on Judge Lord's name, she transformed Christ's dying words into a promise of an amatory Eden, linking Heaven with the "Paradise" enjoyed by Antony and Cleopatra. Are these the words of an impertinent child or of a coy blasphemer? The effect of many of these juxtapositions is not to elevate or illustrate the human situation through scriptural allusion but rather to accommodate the Biblical passage to the human situation, adding merely the spice of humor with no enriching point of analogy. In other words, parody frequently becomes burlesque.

From Emily Dickinson's letters and poems we can piece together a kind of Devil's Dictionary, cataloguing, with what often masquerades as a child's mischievousness, the chief tenets of the creed. For example, the Father and the Son are deftly and outrageously depicted in terms of the Miles Standish-Priscilla-John Alden romance:

> God is a distant — stately Lover —
> Woos, as He states us — by His Son —
> Verily, a Vicarious Courtship —
> "Miles", and "Priscilla", were such an One —
>
> But, lest the Soul — like fair "Priscilla"
> Choose the Envoy — and spurn the Groom —
> Vouches, with hyperbolic archness —
> "Miles", and "John Alden" were Synonyme —
>
> (P 357, I.284)

Elsewhere the "covenant" which binds the Trinity is worked out as a shrewd business transaction: "God broke his contract to his Lamb/ To qualify the Wind." Providence means that "if it be his will that I become a *bear* and bite my fellow men, it will be for the highest good of this fallen and perishing world." Sin is "a distinguished Precipice/ Others must resist." Man is, absurdly, imprisoned with guilt for an unknown and uncommitted sin. Prayer is vain outcry; the Sacrament a cause for either terrified flight or uneasy humor which equates Christ and Santa Claus. Predestination, redemption, atonement, grace, sanctification, election — concepts which supposedly explain our destiny and our hope — are all beyond the reach of human ken.[31]

From the individual's point of view, the question of immortality was the most pressing of religious propositions. To "crumbling men" an "Adamant Estate" presented a comforting prospect, and sometimes she thought that "This World is not Conclusion":

> No vacillating God
> Ignited this Abode
> To put it out —   (P 1599, III.1101)

Yet immortality ("To die — without the Dying / And live — without the Life") was "the hardest Miracle/ Propounded to Belief." All too frequently it seemed "a Dice — a Doubt," even a "Superstition." "Even in Our Lord's ['] that they be with me where I am,' I taste interrogation." Though she might tell herself that the persistence of the riddle is the spur to goad us on, the uncertainty often reduced her to the puzzlement of a lost child.[32]

Biographers have claimed that passing years and the death of friends forced a serene acceptance of immortality, but though at times she found blind faith a necessary refuge, much of the time she would have been satisfied with the stoicism that she admired in Judge Lord, which neither feared extinction nor prized redemption. The insistent question broke from her with every loss.[33] After her father's death she wondered where he was: "Without any body, I keep thinking. What kind can that be?" After Wadsworth's death in 1882: "Lives he in any other world / My faith cannot reply." Later in 1882, after Judge Lord's severe illness she asked: "Is immortality true?" After her mother's death toward the end of the year: "We don't know where she is, though so many tell us." After James F. Clark's death in 1883: "Are you certain there is another life? When overwhelmed to know, I feel that few are sure." After the death of her beloved nephew Gilbert in 1883: " 'Open the Door, open the Door, they are waiting for me,' was Gilbert's sweet command in delirium. *Who* were waiting for him, all we possess we should give to know." After Otis Lord's death in 1884: she "presumed" that his "steadfast heart" was borne "through the Tomb." From her deathbed: "Deity — does He live now?" Her terrors were sublimated into poems which envisioned her own death, her corpse, her funeral,[34] and desperately she would inquire into the last thoughts of dying loved ones in the hope of catching some glint of things beyond.

We know that Emily Dickinson's rejection of doctrine and her doubts concerning immortality were not isolated phenomena. From all sides the most dynamic figures in New England were attacking and destroying the intellectual system which had governed the lives of their ancestors. The Puritan theology had splintered into sharply opposing viewpoints even before the middle of the eighteenth century when Jonathan Edwards, the last great Puritan mind, was writing his theological tracts. A century later no major writer was to speak from within the intellectual framework of New England Christianity. Even Hawthorne and Dickinson, haunted as they were by the Puritan spirit, were too late to rest in "the faith of the fathers," though they could never wholly escape from its shadow. Others were louder in their protests, beating the drums in a campaign of liberation. "Our young people," Emerson intoned, "are diseased with the theological problems of original sin, origin of evil, predestination and the like. . . These are the soul's mumps and measles and whooping cough. . ." For all his mystic insight, even Swedenborg, the modern prophet, was constricted, in Emerson's words, by "the same theologic cramp." Religion, said Thoreau, was the fanning of fears instead of hopes; it was the defamation of God's nature and man's nature by "doctrines of despair." "The wisest man preaches no doctrines . . . Even Christ, we fear, had his scheme, his conformity to tradition, which slightly vitiates his teaching." Worse still for Thoreau — indeed, the greatest infidelity — was the rotten growth of institutionalized churches.

At Christmas 1859, in thanking Mrs. Bowles for the gift of a little book, Emily noted that if the author was poisonous, as she had heard, then she liked the taste of poison.[35] The book, Theodore Parker's *The Two Christmas Celebrations*, is revealing in the light of her endorsement. Parker moved his narrative from the humble simplicity of Jesus' birth through His preaching of individual piety and good will to the corruption of Jesus' example into Christianity, with all its paraphernalia of redemption, resurrection, miracles, devils, heaven, and hell. The "poison" which he asked the reader to swallow was the notion that the example of Christ's life for his followers was an individuality which "broke away from the old established doctrines and forms," for "the best and most religious men were those who had least faith in what was preached and practised as the authorized religion of the land."

Emily understood the force of Thoreau's question: "Can you put mysteries into words? Do you presume to fable of the ineffable?" She knew the force of Emerson's statement of Montaigne's skepticism: "Knowledge is the knowing that we can not know"; "What is the use of pretending to powers that we have not? What is the use of pretending to assurances we have not respecting the other life? . . . If there are conflicting evidences, why not state them?" She understood skepticism all too well and she could not take the easy escape of merely dismissing the problems. She could not ignore the presence of evil or the inhibition of limits, as Emerson tried to do, nor, like Thoreau, declare herself free of the consequences of original sin. Emerson's optimistic assertion that questions of sin and eternity "never presented a practical difficulty to any man, — never darkened any man's road who did not go out of his way to seek them" must have seemed the most fatuous nonsense to her. How could a conscious person blandly declare that "man, though in brothels, or jails, or on gibbets, is on his way to all that is good and true"? How could Emerson not wonder apprehensively what lay beyond the grave? How could Thoreau say that he learned to die from the leaves, which fall "resigned to lie and decay at the foot of the tree, and afford nourishment to new generations"? It was a more difficult world than that — truly a world of conflicting evidences. So "why not state them?" She could not be certain when to commit herself to belief and when to pull back. The poems and letters shift from statement to counterstatement to restatement with a restlessness that would allow her only fleeting ease. Rest would come only with certitude, and on her lonely exploration she would never find the miraculous Fleece that would end the quest. Poe would have understood very well the representation of experience as an expedition to catastrophe:

> Finding is the first Act
> The second, loss,
> Third, Expedition for
> the "Golden Fleece"
>
> Fourth, no Discovery —
> Fifth, no Crew —
> Finally, no Golden Fleece —
> Jason — sham — too.   (P 870, II.647–648)

SEEING NEW ENGLANDLY:
FROM EDWARDS TO EMERSON
TO DICKINSON

Beneath Emily Dickinson's little jokes about being a "Pagan" there lay an honest recognition, but beneath her allusion, just a few years before her death, to her "Puritan Spirit," [1] there lay a recognition equally honest. No commentary on Emily Dickinson can avoid the observation that despite her restlessness she was very much of New England. The crucial question asks precisely in what respects hers was a Puritan spirit in the larger evolution of the American character.

I

The Puritan's "vision" of himself and the cosmos [2] was formulated into theological tenets the truth of which rested not on scriptural authority alone but on the individual's sense of things. To the Puritan, God was the self-existent Being who devised the magnificent harmony of Creation and sustained it in contingent existence while He reigned above in incomprehensible sovereignty. But God's plan had been ruined by man's original sin, through which he lost grace. The loss of grace, that projection of the divine whose indwelling presence united man and nature and God, left man in solitary need and ushered in death, pain, depravity — the consequences of man's descent to a merely natural existence. Blind and impotent, crippled in mind and will, he stood in cringing dependence before an unseen and now angry Jehovah, who could elect to strike him with thunderbolts or to confer through Christ's mediation the grace which, all undeserved, would span the gaping separation, raise man's faculties, and restore him to unity with his God and his world. The Scriptures were God's words to man, through which he could understand the truth of his plight and the nature of his regeneration. Man's duty was to ponder and elucidate God's message and to carry out His Commandments. Hence the single-minded concern of Puritan divines with applying man's reason to God's revelation; and the unrelenting labor to erect a vast theological system on which fallen man could rely and within which he could think and act.

Needless to say, at its best Puritanism amounted to more than an arid rationalism or an abject surrender to formulae. Within the theological structure, the obligation of the individual man strained his stamina to the uttermost. He had to confront the universe starkly and answer within the privacy of his heart all the basic questions: Who am I? What is my relation to the not-me? How must I live in the certitude of death? Have I grounds for hope or not? In this confrontation the noblest Puritans neither winced nor succumbed. On the contrary, within their theology they lived as individuals fully and passionately; universal religious truth and individual human experience were working not at cross-purposes but toward concentricity. One has only to turn to Bradford's *Of Plimmoth Plantation* or Winthrop's "Journal" or Nathaniel Ward or Samuel Sewell or the verse of poets as different as Anne Bradstreet and Edward Taylor to realize with what vigor and passion the Puritan could commit himself, mind and heart and soul, to life. Most splendidly, there is the fierce brightness of Jonathan Edwards, illuminating both worlds. He resolved "to live with all my might, while I do live," and so to strive for heaven "with all the power, might, vigour, and vehemence, yes violence I am capable of." He asserted the importance of the passions and the holiness of religious affections. He loved his wife and God's radiant world, while rejoicing all the more in the "Divine and Supernatural Light."

Only seventy-five years after Edwards' death it seemed to Emerson that the body of doctrine had become a corpse, devoid of feeling or response, stiffened by rigor mortis. What could a living person do but inter the dead? But then he was left to confront the cosmos without even the authority of the Scriptures or the protective framework of established truth. Moreover, Emerson started from a different philosophical viewpoint from Edwards: Emerson's epistemology was not based on Locke's inductive method but on the intuitive perception of the post-Kantian transcendentalists; his metaphysic found German idealism and Oriental mysticism more congenial than Christian dualism.

Nevertheless, Edwards' and Emerson's formulations bespeak continuity as well as change. Like a good New Englander, Emerson also began with a double awareness of things: there was, or seemed to be, Nature and Soul, matter and spirit, not-me and me, Understanding and Reason. There was an "inevitable dualism," and the purpose of life was to resolve the opposition — not in some hypothetical future but here and now. He could admit the appalling impingements and limitations which constituted "Fate"; he could concede that "there is a crack in every thing that God has made"; he could see the world as fragmented and out of joint. But for Emerson the remedy was right at hand. The Fall was an illusion; nor was man helpless and debased, except by choice. Man was the vessel of divinity and need only release his energies; he was "a god in ruins," and could be a god in fact, like Jesus Christ. Man's Fall was only his first realization of himself as an existence apparently distinct, but the process of living was the opening out of one's self to discover "an occult relation" with all other things. In moments of most expansive perception the divine energy flowing from "me" became one again with the divine energy surging from the "not-me." At such times "I am nothing; I see all; the currents of the Universal Being circulate through me; I am part or parcel of God." Each and all, matter and spirit are One.

What had happened over the years[3] was that the masterful synthesis which Edwards represented — that glowing fusion of intellectual and emotional character, that precarious poising of delight in this world against commitment to the next, that careful balance between individual and church — had been split asunder, and the Puritan mind, unable to repair the damage, would not be whole again. Thus, however similar are the axiomatic assumptions of Edwards' "vision" and the "vision" of Emerson, they could hardly have projected more dissimilar views of man's situation. Both men would agree that the individual loses himself in the highest knowledge only through a supra-logical spiritual power which manifests itself in a movement of the affections. Edwards would call that power grace; and Emerson, Reason. Edwards would place its source in God, and Emerson would place it in man. Finally, Edwards would support even the perceptions of grace with a rational system and with a community, while Emerson would leave the self reliant only on intuitive "Reason" and the responsive heart. For Emerson, Reason made each man "full of grace," and instituted a new scheme of "redemption" (though Emerson would not have invoked the theological terms he had so conspicuously shed). Man was god; hence he saved himself; and then earth was heaven. For Edwards heaven was the transcendence of earth; for Emerson it was the fulfillment of earth.

From the beginning there had been in Protestantism the impulse to push the notion of private conscience to its final extreme — namely, unquestioned reliance on individual revelation. In America there had been the related heresies of Anne Hutchinson and Roger Williams and the Friends, and there had been Cotton Mather's concept of "a particular faith" and Solomon Stoddard's awed respect for the unfathomable workings of grace in the individual. For a long time the orthodox had been effective in restraining the tendency to fix on the "inner light" by controlling it within themselves and by driving the heretics out. Ironically, both Edwards and Emerson became, for their respectable contemporaries, irrational enthusiasts. However, while the conservative "Arminians" had successfully stamped out the fires that spread from Edwards' Northampton, their Unitarian grandchildren pitted themselves in a losing effort against the hotheads from Concord. Indeed, the momentum of the rebellious young Turks succeeded in routing a debilitated theological Protestantism and establishing the primacy of personal, innate, and now "secular" vision. Thereby the drama of "salvation," or rather fulfillment, was located in the individual consciousness — a word whose connotations are very different from those of the word "soul." The final step in the transition was the recognition of the poet as the priest and saint and representative man of the new "religion" (he "stands among partial men for the complete man"), and the recognition of the creative imagination as man's divine faculty.

For the Puritans, "a religious heart inevitably translated itself into the formulae of theology; to them the conception of private experience was real, but not of private expression — wherein they differed from modern poets."[4] Although Edwards might have disagreed, Allen Tate has argued that the best poetry is written when the control of the intellectual and religious order of an age is breaking down.[5] Then, says Mr. Tate, the poet — who knows the elements of this order as part of his heritage without being able any longer to accept them unquestioningly — is forced to examine that heritage in terms of his own experience. The shattering of the tradition frees yet directs the energies of the imagination, and the result is magnificent poetry. If Mr. Tate is correct, Emily Dickinson came at the auspicious moment and to precisely the right place. Nurtured in the conservative Connecticut Valley, she not only came to distrust its theology but was personally incapable of logical, not to say theological, thought. System and argument, like the austere New England winter, were too hard and frigid for her, but now, at the crucial period of thaw, she came upon the warm, swelling, swirling notions of the Romantic poet-prophets. In Margaret Fuller's energetic words from the manifesto of the first issue of *The Dial*, Emily Dickinson was merely responding to

the strong current of thought and feeling, which, for a few years past, has led many sincere persons in New England to make new demands on literature, and to reprobate that rigor of our conventions of religion and education, which is turning us to stone, which renounces hope, which looks only backward, which . . . holds nothing so much in horror as new views and the dreams of youth.[6]

2

The testimony of Emily Fowler Ford, one of Emily Dickinson's closest girlhood friends, indicates that as early as the mid-1840's, before the poet had met Benjamin Newton or Henry Vaughan Emmons, the two girls were reading Byron, Lowell, Emerson, Motherwell, and Margaret Fuller's translation of *Günerode*, and Emily Dickinson was particularly "steeped" in Emerson's *Essays*.[7]

In 1847 a series of lectures on the history of literature delivered at Amherst College by a man named John Lord was reported to be scandalously "pantheistic" and "transcendental."

When Professor William Tyler, a neighbor and friend of the Dickinsons, wrote scornfully of the tone of the proceedings, his correspondent replied: "I picture to myself all the grave Prof's of Am. assembled at a transcendental poetical lecture, and I am taken in a very humorous state of mind to say the least . . . Miss Emily should not be absent." Of course, this may not have been our Miss Emily, but the possibility is too intriguing not to mention, especially since Emily would almost certainly have heard the substance of the lectures, even if she herself were not there.[8]

Among Emily's Amherst friends Leonard Humphrey was interested in Wordsworth and Carlyle, and George Gould delivered a prize speech during Commencement Week, 1848, on "Carlyle's 'Dream of Jean Richter.'" Emily's acquaintance with Dr. Josiah G. Holland dates from the early fifties; and Holland, like Higginson later, was a genteel liberal who was interested in "Women in Literature" and had written an article on the subject for the *Springfield Republican*. He stood for a personal "creedless, churchless, ministerless Christianity," and hailed Emerson's thought as "a chain of brilliant ideas strung as thickly as Wethersfield onions when packed for export." In 1881 Emily warmly recalled to Mrs. Holland that when she had first heard her husband pray, she had thought that she felt "a different God" who was a friend.[9]

Emily gave some idea of Emerson's influence upon her own thought in her comments on the *Poems, Representative Men,* and the Holmes biography, and in several allusions to his "immortal" poems.[10] Emerson spoke in Amherst in 1855 on "A Plea for the Scholar," in 1857 on "The Beautiful in Rural Life," in 1879 on "Superlative or Mental Temperance," and led off a course of lectures in 1865 with "Social Aims." That he met with small crowds and little enthusiasm, even as late as his lecture of 1879 (by which time he was something of a national monument), indicates the extent to which Emily's interest outran that of her Amherst neighbors. Although there is no evidence that she attended any of these lectures, she must have listened from a distance, and after the 1857 visit, when Emerson stayed at the house next door with Austin and Sue, she wrote breathlessly to her sister-in-law: "It must have been as if he had come from where dreams are born!" In her last years she copied out several scraps of Emerson's verse. This was a special tribute, for she rarely copied the words of other poets, even her favorites; and the attribution to Emerson of the anonymously published "Success" (the only poem of hers to appear in print outside of a newspaper during her lifetime) must have amused and delighted her.[11] She wrote of the severe shock which Emerson's death dealt her in April 1882. Since the Reverend Wadsworth had died just a few weeks before, death had struck down within a single month the men who symbolized and supported the two sides of her divided spirit.

For Emily Dickinson's indebtedness to Thoreau we have fewer hard facts to point to than in the case of Emerson, but circumstantial evidence intimates a great deal (though the influence here was somewhat later and so less directly formative than that of Emerson). The Dickinson library copies of *Letters to Various Persons* and *A Week on the Concord and Merrimack* and the two copies of *Walden* are dated from the middle sixties, but she might have read any of them earlier. Besides, she must have read the essays which appeared in the pages of the *Atlantic* during 1862: "Walking," "Autumnal Tints," "Wild Apples," and others. And her remark to Sue and Austin on a seaside vacation in 1865 — "Was the Sea cordial? Kiss him for Thoreau" — shows that she knew the recently issued *Cape Cod*. Her writing is filled with scattered remarks which suggest Thoreau's influence: " 'My Country, 'tis of Thee,' has always meant the Woods — to me — 'Sweet Land of Liberty,' I trust is your own — "; "The fire-bells are oftener now, almost, than the church-bells. Thoreau would wonder which did the most harm." There is, too, the charming anecdote of the lady who, having been "recently introduced in the family by marriage," was brought for the first time to Edward Dickinson's house to meet her new relatives. When by chance she "quoted some sentence from Thoreau's writings, Miss Dickinson, recognizing it, hastened to press her hand as she said, 'From this time we are acquainted;' and this was the beginning of a friendship that lasted till the death of the poetess." [12] Emily must have felt a deep kinship with Thoreau for a passing reference to provoke so spontaneous and wholehearted a response to a stranger.

As for other Transcendentalists, she read some of Theodore Parker and later O. B. Frothingham's biography of Parker; and she knew enough about William Ellery Channing to use a verse of his as the basis for a poem of her own (P1234, III.858). But since specific information is so meager, the full extent of her knowledge of what was going on in Concord can best be suggested through her own words. Curiously enough it is the conclusion of a comic valentine which indicates how clearly she had absorbed, as early as 1850, the essential features of Transcendentalism — the optimism, the emphasis on experimentation and originality, the sense of social purpose, the metaphysical and mystical speculations, the pulse of rhythm and imagery:

But the world is sleeping in ignorance and error, sir, and we must be crowing cocks, and singing larks, and a rising sun to awake her; or else we'll pull society up to the roots, and plant it in a different place. We'll build Alms-houses, and transcendental State prisons, and scaffolds — we will blow out the sun, and the moon, and encourage invention. Alpha shall kiss Omega — we will ride up the hill of glory — Hallelujah, all hail! [13]

The shock of Transcendentalism had been registered on the American consciousness even as far as Amherst; Brook Farm and

The Dial were experiments now defunct, but they were events of such import that henceforth New England could not think without taking into account what they had stood for. In *The Blithedale Romance* (1852) Hawthorne would tell of Hollingsworth's schemes for penal reform; in *Walden* (1854) Thoreau would "brag as lustily as chanticleer in the morning . . . if only to wake my neighbors up," for "only that day dawns to which we are awake. There is more day to dawn. The sun is but a morning-star." Emily Dickinson's words of 1850 had already caught much of the imagery and fanfare.

3

The early letters of Emily's correspondence record the development of her imagination and her growing sense of poetic mission. From the first she welcomed the opportunity for "improving" a situation. In her earliest extant letter, written in 1842 when she was twelve, she told Austin of sleeping alone and imagining deliciously dire perils, then went on to describe Austin's hens which "will be so large that you cannot perceive them with the naked Eye when you get home," and narrated the theft of an egg by "a skonk . . . or else a hen In the shape of a skonk and I dont know which." [14] These capricious childhood fantasies are not remarkable in themselves, except to indicate the play of fancy which she was soon to apply to increasingly serious purpose.

At about the time when she was discovering some of the new writers, she indulgently warned Abiah Root about the enchainment of the free spirit; and after loosing a flutter of metaphors on another occasion she paused to intone to her professing friend in sly mockery:

Now my dear friend, let me tell you that these last thoughts are fictions — vain imaginations to lead astray foolish young women. They are flowers of speech, they both *make*, and *tell* deliberate falsehoods,

64

avoid them as the snake . . . Honestly tho', a snake bite is a serious matter, and there can't be too much said, or done about it . . . *I* love those little green ones that slide around by your shoes in the grass — and make it rustle with their elbows — they are rather my favorites on the whole, but I would'nt influence *you* for the world! [15]

With a wave of the hand she had charmed the venomous serpent into a harmless grass snake, which was, after all, her favorite sort of reptile. The nimble feat of verbal prestidigitation was to admit the sins of fancy and then absolve them through the fancy's ingenuity.

In April 1850 (the year Emily received Emerson's *Poems* from Benjamin Newton) she wrote Jane Humphrey a long letter which, underneath all the inarticulate confusion, bespoke a special sense of dedication. The importance of the passage to the emergence of the poet — it may even be roughly analogous to the moment of consecration in Wordsworth's *Prelude* — merits its quotation in full:

I would whisper to you in the evening of many, and curious things — and by the lamps eternal read your thoughts and response in your face, and find out what you thought about me, and what I have done, and am doing . . . I have dared to do strange things — bold things, and have asked no advice from any — I have heeded beautiful tempters, yet do not think I am wrong . . . Oh Jennie, it would relieve me to . . . confess what *you only* shall know, an experience bitter, and sweet, but the sweet did so beguile me — and life has had an aim, and the world has been too precious for your poor — and striving sister! The winter was all one dream, and the spring has not yet waked me, I would *always* sleep, and dream, and it never should turn to morning, so long as night is so blessed. What do you weave from all these threads . . . I hope belief is not wicked, and assurance, and perfect trust — . . . do you dream from all this what I mean? Nobody *thinks* of the joy, nobody *guesses* it, to all appearance old things are engrossing, and new ones are not revealed, but there *now* is nothing old, things are budding, and springing, and singing, and you rather think you are in a green grove, and it's branches that go, and come.[16]

Twice she asks the momentous question: what do you make of all this? Momentous indeed was the implication of the painful transition to a sweet new life and a renewed world. Perhaps it was a dream, as it seemed at first, but then the dream of joyous vision was better than hopeless reality. Excitement, mingled with reticence, blurred the point in a whirl of words, but even in her most intimate moments she would refer only obliquely to that "attitude toward the Universe, so precisely my own," for which she had relinquished the Christian "Vision of John at Patmos." [17]

Now she was bold enough to appropriate to herself the title of poet. In 1851 she spoke of "the fancy that we are the only poets, and everyone else is *prose*." A few months later, while the rest of the family was at church, she conducted her own service for Sue in her heart and only regretted the lack of things "which I may poetize" for "this sweet Sabbath of our's." In 1853 she good-naturedly chided Austin, her "Brother Pegasus," for writing verses, because as a poet in her own right she was reluctant to share the laurels with him. To the Hollands she identified herself with the village poet in Longfellow's *Kavanagh*. A sermon (given by Professor E. A. Park of the Andover Theological Seminary) on "the importance of Aesthetic in connection with Religious and Moral Culture" brought this exclamation: "I never heard anything like it, and dont expect to again . . ." By 1854 Sue's persistence about her sister-in-law's unregenerate state pressed too hard, but in her wounded reply Emily would not compromise her new calling: "Sue — you can go or stay — There is but one alternative . . . I have lived by this. It is the lingering emblem of the Heaven I once dreamed . . ." [18] If in Sue's eyes she had abandoned Christ for Satan, it was too bad; her decision was unalterable, and, as if to emphasize her new role, she finished the letter with a poem. Most frequently now her signature read "Emilie," which some critics have taken as the mask of the child-poet (in the Blake-Wordsworth-Emerson tradition) but which might just as well be read as the sign of the new poet enjoying the embellishment of verbal curlicues.

During the fifties the letters began to mention and display a concern for style.[19] The struggle for stylistic effects grew out of the necessity to make a language adequate to the more ambitious descriptions of nature that she was attempting. They are often keenly perceived and crisply phrased, and even the exuberant excesses are interesting as a novice's explorations of the resources of her medium. To Sue in Maryland she mused: the moon "looks like a fairy tonight, sailing around the sky in a little silver gondola with stars for gondoliers. I asked her to let me ride a little while ago — and told her I would *get out* when she got as far as Baltimore, but she only smiled to herself and went sailing on." The autumn countryside which she dispatched to the city-bound Austin is more finely realized:

I have tried to delay the frosts, I have coaxed the fading flowers, I thought I *could* detain a few of the crimson leaves until you had smiled upon them, but their companions call them and they cannot stay away — you will find the blue hills, Austin, with the autumnal shadows silently sleeping on them, and there will be a glory lingering round the day, so you'll know autumn has been here, and the *setting sun* will tell you . . . The earth looks like some poor old lady who by dint of pains has bloomed e'en till *now*, yet in a forgetful moment a few silver hairs from out her cap come stealing, and she tucks them back so hastily and thinks nobody *sees*.

At the end of this message to her Brother Pegasus she set down (unobtrusively as rhymed prose) the first serious poem sent in a letter. In 1852 we find this imagistic scene: "the shy little birds would say chirrup, chirrup in the tall cherry trees, and if our dresses rustled, hop frightened away; and there used to be some farmer cutting down a tree in the woods, and you and I, sitting there, could hear his sharp ax ring." In 1856 her cousin John Graves received a prose lyric whose landscape and logic are now completely imaginative: "Ah John — *Gone?* Then I lift the lid to my box of Phantoms, and lay another in, unto the Resurrection — Then will I gather in *Paradise*, the blossoms fallen here, and on the shores of the sea of Light, seek my missing sands." [20]

By 1858, after some years of apprenticeship, she felt sufficiently sure of her sight and insight and of her technique to begin recopying verses and preserving them in bound packets. The letters and the rapidly expanding body of poems displayed increasing control of theme, image, and diction. Under the stress of emotional crisis she composed more than five hundred poems in 1862 and 1863. Nor were they all written to relieve the pressure of pain; there is in the nature poetry a deepening wonder at the awesome beauty of the world. The verse of these years includes nature poems, poems of states of feeling, poems about poetry and the poet, poems about love, death, and immortality — in short, all the major patterns of theme and imagery. By the early sixties the design of Emily Dickinson's art was set; the rest of her poetic life was an elaboration and a perfection.

4

The critic can cull the poems and letters for a catalogue of transcendental "doctrines" which the poet had, for the moment at any rate, espoused. If Emerson referred to the world as "a divine dream, from which we may presently awake," Dickinson said: "Reality is a dream from which but a portion of mankind have yet waked . . ." If Emerson urged self-knowledge and self-reliance, Dickinson exhorted her poetic persona:

> Soto! Explore thyself!
> Therein thyself shalt find
> The "Undiscovered Continent" —
> No Settler had the Mind.   (P 832, II.631)[*]

[*] Reprinted by permission of Houghton Mifflin Co. from *Emily Dickinson Face to Face* by Martha Dickinson Bianchi (Boston, 1932).

And:

> Lad of Athens, faithful be
> To Thyself,
> And Mystery —
> All the rest is Perjury —   (P 1768, III.1183)

If Emerson perceived the correspondence which made the world the emblematic "web of God," Dickinson saw things as "trembling Emblems" and felt the movements of an unseen Weaver. If Emerson's position rested on the divine faculty of Intuition, Dickinson claimed "Glee intuitive" as "the gift of God." [21]

Anyone who has given Emerson and Dickinson a thorough reading can indulge in the game of finding more cases in point, but such analogues could be misleading if they are insisted upon too rigidly, because the words of a lyric poet like Emily Dickinson express not philosophic generalizations but the measure of a particular moment. On the other hand, the critic cannot resign himself to an aimless chronological reading of almost 1800 lyrics. He must try to perceive in the shifting record of successive moments the salient recurrences, relations, and patterns without reducing the poet's mind to an abstraction. And so we must watch Emily approach Emerson by a dark and circuitous path.

Wherever Emily Dickinson's mental processes may have led, they began with an intolerable sense of emptiness which drove her to project as concrete evidence of her incompleteness the loss of childhood, father, mother, lover. She could list childhood and the dead among the "Things that never can come back"; she could even enumerate the things lost with childhood. But in all honesty she had to add: "But is that all I have lost — memory drapes her Lips." [22] These losses — genuine and heartfelt — were at least definable and hence bearable, but what seemed excruciating was the fact that almost the first act of the mind was an awareness of isolation. Edwards would have attributed this knowledge to original sin, and Emerson to the separation of the object from the Oversoul. But Emily Dickinson's was a characteristically personal response: all she knew was that she had to manage somehow from day to day, eating and sleeping and speaking and acting in the hollowness of the void:

> A loss of something ever felt I —
> The first that I could recollect
> Bereft I was — of what I knew not
>
> (P 959, II.694)

The poem does not specify what was lost; all she could say was that she was bereft of something in and of herself, something so private that it belonged to her as an individual and would make her, as she was not now, a whole person.

> I cannot buy it — 'tis not sold —
> There is no other in the World —
> Mine was the only one   (P 840, II.635)

Before anything — faith, love, happiness — were possible, before she could give or take or act, the unknown factor had somehow to be found:

> If I could find it Anywhere
> I would not mind the journey there
> Though it took all my store   (P 840, II.636)

So hers was a quest through an interior waste land, trackless and guideless, without even the name of the missing treasure. She could call it what she would — friend, lover, mother, father, "Golden Fleece," God — but these names could never contain the dark immensity of "Missing All." Life began with "Missing All"; and its trek through time seemed a dreary repetition of losses, of missing in turn each of the things most dear, until "Parting is all we know of heaven,/ And all we need of hell." In this private hell the lonely mourner "walked among the children." [23]

Even Satan, however, soon found that hell had its own compensations — the stimulus to yearn and struggle and resist. And in her own way Emily Dickinson came to draw sustenance from the substance of her sorrow. "I always try to think in any disappointment that had I been gratified, it had been sadder still, and I weave from such suppositions, *at times*, considerable consolation; consolation upside down as I am pleased to call it." "Consolation upside down" gave way sometimes to a brighter possibility: "To miss you, Sue, is power"; "Possession — has a sweeter chink/ Upon a Miser's Bar." Nor was she seeking solace in futile paradox; she was stating, flatly and deliberately, her recognition of the only grounds on which life without delusion was possible: "The stimulus of Loss makes most Possession mean." [24]

How could loss be power beyond possession? Because loss made us desire, made us project an object for our desire, made us strain urgently toward it. What we lacked we wanted, and if we lacked all, we wanted all. Fulfillment was static, like eternity; but desire was a process, and was therefore the prerequisite and condition of human life. At times, even, desire found response; for a moment we glimpsed what we wanted to see, grasped what we wanted to hold. Afterward, these fleeting moments of fulfillment provided the stimulus for the continuation of the process. Although we know that possession "is past the instant/ We achieve the Joy," we can accept life for the memory of past moments, the ecstasy of the present, the anticipation of the future:

> Satisfaction — is the Agent
> Of Satiety —
> Want — a quiet Comissary
> For Infinity.   (P 1036, II. 735)

In other words, man's littleness was, in a strange way, the condition for his greatness, and his limitations pointed him toward infinity. Edwards would have regarded this thesis as untenable, and Emerson would have found it morbid. There is something peculiarly modern about it. Nietzsche defined the tragic sense as the assertion of the will to live in the face of death and the inexhaustible joy which that assertion releases. Yeats wrote in his autobiography, "We begin to live when we have conceived of life as tragedy." In his version of *Women of Trachis* Ezra Pound had the dying and thwarted Herakles exclaim: "what/ SPLENDOUR, IT ALL COHERES." In *The Myth of Sisyphus* Albert Camus rejects suicide and chooses life despite its absurdity. Emily Dickinson, who spoke of "Confident Despair," would have understood these expressions of tragic joy. It was knowledge of "this brief Tragedy of Flesh" that made life precious; it was acceptance of loss and defeat that made an unexpected moment of vision into "that bright tragic thing." [25]

For this reason "Life never loses it's startlingness, however assailed," or — to state the idea in personal terms — "Who never lost, are unprepared / A Coronet to find!" [26] The crown's shining and full circle did descend on us, if only in momentary glory, and life was not only possible but beautiful as long as there were times when the void was filled with abundance. In "Burnt Norton" T. S. Eliot restated the moment for a waste-land century, but it is very much the same event:

> Dry the pool, dry concrete, brown edged,
> And the pool was filled with water out of sunlight,
> And the lotos rose, quietly, quietly,
> The surface glittered out of heart of light, . . .
> Then a cloud passed, and the pool was empty.*

If many of the Romantic prophets did not share her experience of darkness, they confirmed and defined for her the experience of overwhelming brightness. At its most sublime intensity, the momentary incandescence consumed the categories of human Understanding and held all in its illumination. In Emerson's

* T. S. Eliot, "Burnt Norton," in *Four Quartets* (New York: Harcourt, Brace & World Inc., 1943), p. 4.

words, with the movements of Reason, "there is the incoming or the receding of God: that is all we can affirm; and we can show neither how nor why." In Dickinson's image the manifestation was "a Blossom of the Brain," "the Spirit fructified." The cessation of such epiphanies would be "the Funeral of God," for each of these sublime moments was indeed "a cordial interview / With God" — not, she told her nephew Ned, the unseen Jehovah in epaulettes but another Eleusinian Deity who revealed Himself in an overpowering efflux of life. Heaven vested itself for each man, and for the sake of those incarnations one could endure the residue of life and "entertain Despair." [27] For Thoreau they had the same vitalizing function:

> Within the circuit of this plodding life,
> There enter moments of an azure hue,
> Untarnished fair as is the violet
>
> . . . .
>
> So by God's cheap economy made rich
> To go upon my winter's task again. [28]

So vital was the illumination that Emily tried time and again to make stubborn words render some sense of the glory: it was God's intrusion through which He was known and through which He confounded "Time's possibility"; it was "Eternity — obtained — in Time"; it was "Reversed Divinity," which, falling like a thunderbolt, transfixed mortality "in a moment of Deathlessness." [29] The quatrain below suggests metrically the moment's uncertain approach which reaches climactic force in the last leaping phrase:

> 'Tis this — invites — appalls — endows —
> Flits — glimmers — proves — dissolves —
> Returns — suggests — convicts — enchants —
> Then — flings in Paradise —   (P 673, II.520)

For most of the Romantics, however transcendental, Nature served as intermediary between self and Deity, as the meeting place of the new "religion." Among Emily Dickinson's earliest poems there is a splendid evocation of a very special summer's day (P 122, I.88), and many such poems followed over the years. At the beginning of her correspondence with Higginson, when she was trying to make him understand her "vision," she spoke in one letter alone of the "noiseless noise in the Orchard," of the stopping of breath "in the core of the Woods," of the sight of the chestnut tree that made the skies blossom for her, and finally of the wood visited by Angels. During her childhood her religious elders had forbidden her to enter the woods because of the venomous snake and the poisonous flowers (remember her warning to Abiah Root about the snake and the flowers of the imagination), but on later investigation despite their warnings she had found in Nature only an angelic visitation.[30]

Nature was precious because it was the material medium through which God or the Life Spirit touched man and through which man touched Him or It. Several poems invent images for the indefinable fusion of matter and spirit:

> 'Tis Compound Vision —
> Light — enabling Light —
> The Finite — furnished
> With the Infinite —
> Convex — and Concave Witness —
> Back — toward Time —
> And forward —
> Toward the God of Him —   (P 906, II.666)

Elsewhere she wrote that the ear could not hear without the "Vital Word" that "came all the way from Life to me," nor could the eye see without divine light. During these visitations dust and Deity, time and eternity, were one, like Eliot's moment neither in time nor out of time, neither flesh nor fleshless.[31]

Man was by no means impotent in the process. Did not his openness, his striving for self-transcendence, indicate something in himself that answered to Spirit? Light, she said, enabled

74

Light; for God to show Himself, we must be able to see. In these supreme moments our cringing souls, covert in the void, did emerge, did in turn show ourselves, did move and expand, so that we ourselves became microscopic incarnations, like "Holy Ghosts in Cages."[32] For the soul exists only in the body, and the body acts only under the soul's impulsion. Or, in poetic imagery:

> The Music in the Violin
> Does not emerge alone
> But Arm in Arm with Touch, yet Touch
> Alone — is not a Tune —
> The Spirit lurks within the Flesh
> Like Tides within the Sea
> That make the Water live, estranged
> What would the Either be?   (P 1576, III.1086)

Nevertheless, like all occurrences in the material order, these "sumptuous moments" went as inexplicably as they came: "Not of detention is Fruition," or, as Frost was to say, "Nothing gold can stay."[33] Despite his ebullient optimism, even Emerson had to admit that in the present state of things Reason's grasp was only momentary: "Like a bird which alights nowhere, but hops perpetually from bough to bough, is the Power which abides in no man and no woman, but for a moment speaks from this one, and for another moment from that one." Emily Dickinson endeavored mightily to accept joy's brevity as part of the process which impelled life to further inspiration. In the following poem the verses, seesawing back and forth in syntax and sound, suggest the oscillation from loss to recovery, from resonant correspondence back to hollow isolation:

> Image of Light, Adieu —
> Thanks for the interview —
> So long — so short —
> Preceptor of the whole —
> Coeval Cardinal —
> Impart — Depart —   (P 1556, III.1072)

In the whole span of the New England tradition, from Bradford and Winthrop and Edwards to Emerson and Dickinson and
later to Eliot and Frost, individual experience finally focused and
rested upon the pivotal moments of revelation and insight — the
moments of divine manifestation and human vision. This union
— however insecure — in which the individual lost himself in
totality is the sole end of that Augustinian strain of piety which
Perry Miller saw as the bright heart of Puritanism. "Without it
individual life was a burden; with it living became richness and
joy." But while Christians see regeneration as the moment of
grace, "other people have found other names for the experience:
to lovers it is love, to mystics it is ecstasy, to poets inspiration." [34]
Edwards called men to the "Great Awakening"; Emerson smiled
in the calm assurance of Reason's ever-expanding sway; and in
Four Quartets Eliot — that Puritan misplaced in the Midwest,
who moved through Boston back to orthodoxy in the Church
that his forebears had abandoned — composed a masterful meditation on "the still point of the turning world." But Emily Dickinson, somewhat after Emerson and before Eliot, could not ar-
rive at the peace and assurance that they found at the ends of
divergent paths. In the face of conflicting evidences her problem,
like Frost's, was "what to make of a diminished thing," and her
response, like his, was "to get now and then elated." For a poet
she was; and, in some senses of the words, a lover and a mystic
as well. What remains, therefore, is to see what she made of and
with her fitful vision.

5

If transcendence comes only to individuals and only in time
and space, these moments of personal revelation must be made
to shape the totality of meaning and of experience. The conquer-
ing of time through time of which Eliot spoke was possible only
if the instant's revelation-vision was fixed in a world of flux,

drawing time and space into perspective around itself and defining the design of faith. The center of light projects the encircling design on all things, and sustains the design through time and perhaps (who knows?) through eternity. If Christian theology no longer provided viable terms to formulate the design, the new "religion" would have to create a new vision; if the discarding of heaven left only earth as the arena of experience, the poet-priest would have to refashion the perception of the here and now.

In "New Views of Christianity, Society, and the Church," [35] Orestes Brownson insisted that he was beginning the process of redefinition within the existing ecclesiastical organization, but the force of his thought carried him and others far beyond. He defined the religious dilemma of the nineteenth century in terms of the interaction of Materialism and Spiritualism. In the intensity of its genesis Christianity had fused the two modes of thinking and living into a dynamic unity. The Middle Ages had erred in an inordinate Spiritualism which scourged the flesh, fanatically blinded to its inherent goodness and beauty. The Protestant reaction swung wrongheadedly to Materialism, so that the only spiritual elements in religion since the Reformation were clinging vestiges of the medieval Church. Now that these had gradually fallen away, the last and supreme expression of Protestant Materialism was the Unitarians' gross and bloated complacency. Christianity could survive, Brownson concluded, only with a resurgence of the primal energy which would again join both orders — matter and spirit, nature and heaven, body and soul — into an organic whole.

In "A Discourse of Matters Pertaining to Religion" [36] Theodore Parker invoked the same dialectic with slightly different labels and pushed the argument further — in fact, out of the Christian context. According to Parker, Naturalism made a substantial distinction between creation and Creator; it envisioned man in Nature, with God "but *transiently* present and active" at the moment of creation, "not *immanently* present and active" from instant to instant. Without God's immanence man could know only naturally through his human intellect; and the Naturalist train of argument soon propelled man into "the Doubt of Hume, the Selfishness of Paley, the coarse materialism of Hobbes," and the rationalism of the Deists and the Unitarians. Supernaturalism also conceived creation as separate from God but insisted that man could know only through God's special intervention and express commands; and this train of argument soon debased man into the superstition of miracles, sacraments, churches, heaven, and hell. However, Parker's argument ran, there was a third approach — Spiritualism, or the Natural-Religious View — which superseded both these partial and divisive views; it eliminated the materiality of the one and the necromancy of the other. Its great synthesis recognized the "connection between God and the soul, as between light and the eye, sound and the ear, food and the palate, truth and the intellect, beauty and the imagination." The authority of the Natural-Religious View, therefore, rested on the "religious consciouness" of "free and conscious men," and its revelation was the perception of the glorious coherence of all things in the immanent Godhead.

Thoreau eliminated the clumsy labels and abstractions of Brownson and Parker to catch the smack and sting of the concrete experience: "I see, smell, taste, hear, feel, that everlasting Something to which we are allied, at once our maker, our abode, our destiny, our very Selves . . ."; "I explore, too, with pleasure, the sources of the myriad sounds which crowd the summer noon, and which seem the very grain and stuff of which eternity is made." His celebration of "a natural Sabbath" was the prayer "for no higher heaven than the pure senses can furnish, a *purely* sensuous life." For "may we not *see* God? . . . Is not Nature, rightly read, that of which she is commonly taken to be the symbol merely? . . . What is it, then, to educate but to develop these divine germs called the senses?" When the senses operated freely, heaven took place all around us, and multiplicity blended into the one divine articulation of Nature.

There was in Emily Dickinson a similar inclination of mind and heart. Whether or not she derived it from reading Brownson and Parker and Thoreau, her response to her own religious dilemma had much in common with theirs. In a letter to the Hollands she had expressed her love of "'time and sense' — and fading things, and things that do *not* fade." [37] It was hard to love time and sense, unless she could somehow transmute fading things into unfading permanence. She could sometimes hope for, sometimes believe in, heaven, and then she accepted earth as a preparation for immortality.[38] But so uncertain a trust was no basis for a life's experience.

The stirrings of a new trust are suggested in these lines:

> The worthlessness of Earthly things
> The Ditty * is that Nature Sings —
> And then — enforces their delight
> Till Synods ** are inordinate —
>
> (P 1373, III.947)

* Alternate word: Sermon   ** Alternate phrase: Zion is

Viewed rightly, the crumbling impermanence of things was lost in the incandescence which illuminated them as it consumed them to ashes. Overpowered by splendor, "I'm half tempted to take my seat in that Paradise of which the good man writes, and begin forever and ever *now*, so wondrous does it seem." Since her vision of nature lay beyond and above the temptation to heaven, she could claim to be luckier than God Himself: "If God had been here this summer, and seen the things that I have seen — I guess that He would think His Paradise superfluous." Often Heaven seemed "a fictitious Country": merely a name for "what I cannot reach," a designation for the furthest extension of experience to an unknown but intuited absolute. Eternity, therefore, was here, not there, if one were but worthy of the vision, and the vision of Heaven below came to replace that of "Papa above." Though "the time to live is frugal," it is sufficient, for "each of us has the skill of life." That is, since each "gives or takes heaven in corporeal person," we can see Nature as Heaven and Heaven in Nature simply by being true to our best selves.[39]

Weighing earth against a doubtful "Heaven to come," she summed up her choice with Yankee shrewdness in an aphorism that reads like Franklin pronouncing through Emerson: "A Savior in a Nut, is sweeter to the grasp than ponderous Prospectives." In the same vein she adapted another folk adage, using Poor Richard's pragmatism to ponder the choice between the temporal world and celestial eternity *:

> I cannot help esteem
>
> The "Bird within the Hand"
> Superior to the one
> The "Bush" may yield me
> Or may not
> Too late to choose again.　(P 1012, II.726)

As a matter of fact, the old terms of distinction might audaciously be reversed: "To be human is more than to be divine, for when Christ was divine, he was uncontented till he had been human." [40] So she would not be the proud wren who vainly sought "a home too high" but rather the lark who

---

* Cf. Frost's maxim, "Earth is still our fate" (*In the Clearing*, New York: Holt, Rinehart & Winston, 1962, p. 52), or the famous lines from "Birches":

> May no fate wilfully misunderstand me
> And half grant what I wish and snatch me away
> Not to return. Earth's the right place for love:
> I don't know where it's likely to go better.

(From *Complete Poems of Robert Frost*. Copyright 1916, 1921, 1923 by Holt, Rinehart and Winston, Inc. Copyright 1942, 1944, 1945 by Robert Frost. Reprinted by permission of Holt, Rinehart and Winston, Inc.).

> is not ashamed
> To build upon the ground
> Her modest house —
>
> Yet who of all the throng
> Dancing around the sun
> Does so rejoice?   (P 143, I.102–3)

The assumption underlying her moments of exultation was not so much that earth as earth was superior to heaven but that earth was heaven, that indeed as Emerson and Thoreau had said, "the 'Supernatural,' was only the Natural, disclosed." [41] In the following poem the structure dramatically conveys the meaning. The statement of the first line — concise, declarative — stands out from the subsequent verses, grammatically tangled and blurred by the recurrence of negatives:

> The Fact that Earth is Heaven — *
> Whether Heaven is Heaven or not
> If not an Affidavit
> Of that specific Spot
> Not only must confirm us
> That it is not for us
> But that it would affront us
> To dwell in such a place —   (P 1408, III.977)

"The Fact that Earth is Heaven"; in other poems "Universe" and "Firmament" and "Deity" become interchangeable alternatives. In her favorite metaphor of house and home — suggesting, as always, that odd Dickinson combination of coziness and awe — she called Nature a haunted house, a mystic house, God's house [42]: the lost Father in Heaven found in His neighborhood lodgings.

---

* Similarly, but much more skeptically, the only God that Frost will admit is the principle of matter penetrated by thought: the "God of the machine," the spirit working "in substantiation" in "the mixture mechanic" (*In the Clearing*, New York: Holt, Rinehart & Winston, Inc. 1962, pp. 49, 57, 58).

The vision of the earth-heaven conferred, at least for those moments, a total acceptance of the natural order of time and process. "Time," cried Emily, "why Time was all I wanted!" [43] With the great Romantic poets she celebrated the mysterious and vital process of growth in which self realized itself in cosmic unity.[44] Time was preferable to eternity, "for the one is still, but the other moves." Immortality was an "ablative estate" which carried us from the dynamic drama of experience, and death's encroachment, which alone kept life from being perfect (that is, from being eternity), nonetheless provided the pressure which made life the more intensely experienced, the more frugally felt. The process — for Dickinson as for Wordsworth, Shelley, Keats, Emerson, and Thoreau — made the world "Fairer though Fading." Besides, the individual process contained and revealed the pattern: to Thoreau's "The revolution of the seasons — is a great and steady flow," Emily added: "Changelessness is Nature's change." [45] So with the acceptance of change and death, the circle of the seasons could become for each of us the unwinding disclosure of heaven. Matter and Spirit, concrete and universal, are the same:

> "Nature" is what we see —
> The Hill — the Afternoon —
> Squirrel — Eclipse — the Bumble bee —
> Nay — Nature is Heaven —
> Nature is what we hear —
> The Bobolink — the Sea —
> Thunder — the Cricket —
> Nay — Nature is Harmony —　　(P 668, II.515)

The force which swept through the world, animating matter into heaven, is sometimes symbolized in the spontaneous harmony of bird-song, but more often in the breath of the wind.[46] Emerson spoke of "the currents of the Universal Being," and Thoreau wrote, "In enthusiasm we undulate to the divine spiritus — as the lake to the wind." In Emily Dickinson's world, too, the wind was the Spiritus Sanctus, unseen but felt in all its operations: "The Wind didn't come from the Orchard — today — / Further than that — "; or, "A Murmur in the Trees — to note — / Not loud enough — for Wind — "; or:

> Exhiliration is the Breeze
> That lifts us from the Ground
> And leaves us in another place
> Whose statement is not found —
>
> (P 1118, II.786)

The culmination of the wind's sweep is a sudden and momentary breathlessness: "When Winds take Forests in their Paws — / The Universe — is still." Suspended in stillness, we open eyes and heart, and we see and know. The event was thus double: outward and inward, revelation and vision, "The Capsule of the Wind / The Capsule of the Mind." [47]

Those climactic capsule moments are most often symbolized in "Lightning — and the Sun — " In Emerson's phrase, revelation traveled "like a thunderbolt to the centre," and repeatedly in Dickinson poems [48] the lightning, striking to the center with light so bright as to be borne for only a flashing second, illuminated all the landscape for her stunned and reeling consciousness. Sometimes she softened the remembrance of the impact by domesticating the lightning image to "yellow feet" or "electric Mocassin" or "a yellow Fork / From Tables in the sky," but she had felt, in ravished awe, the slamming, blinding force. Thunder-stricken like Ahab, but shaken to life and not to death, she saw things "Not yet suspected — but for Flash / And Click — and Suddenness"; and so she "would not exchange the Bolt / For all the rest of Life." Considered in their fullness, these spots of time seemed "torrid Noons," [49] and noon became a major image for their concentric radiance: [50]

You'll know it — as you know 'tis Noon —
By Glory —
As you do the Sun —
By Glory — (P 420, I.326)

Even when Emily Dickinson tried to conjure up a conception of heaven as it was or would be, she could imagine only the natural order extended through time and space. "Forever — is composed of Nows": "not a different time," but a perfected time, an Arcadian Golden Age where "Sun constructs perpetual Noon," where "perfect Seasons wait," where "Consciousness — is Noon." [51]

A Nature be
Where Saints, and our plain going Neighbor
Keep May! (P 977, II.706)

On the other hand the peerless moments revealed earth as Eden before the Fall — Nature perfected to Paradise. If heaven is Arcadia, Eden is heaven. An early poem tells a charming parable about a lost, frost-bitten Puritan flower (a floral variant of the image of herself as a little girl locked out in the cold) who found an unfallen Eden aglow with summer: [52]

As if some little Arctic flower
Upon the polar hem —
Went wandering down the Latitudes
Until it puzzled came
To continents of summer —
To firmaments of sun —
To strange, bright crowds of flowers —
And birds, of foreign tongue!
I say, As if this little flower
To Eden, wandered in —
What then? Why nothing,
Only, your inference therefrom! (P 180, I.132)

One inference is that under the thrust of that "bright" strain of the Romantic spirit of which Wordsworth and Scott are good examples in England, and Bryant, Emerson, and Whitman in America, Emily Dickinson was able to break open the dark inner void to a shining world outside in which, paradoxically, she could both lose and fulfill herself. We dwell in Eden every day, she said, would we but open our eyes, for "Paradise is of the option," is "always eligible." "Not — 'Revelation' — 'tis — that waits, / But our unfurnished eyes." To the poet's eyes " 'Eden' a'nt so lonesome / As New England used to be!" [53]

Once again it is very easy to underestimate the complexity of Emily Dickinson's mind by fastening too exclusively on one aspect of it. Although her rhetorical question "With the Kingdom of Heaven on his knee, could Mr Emerson hesitate?" is a transcendentalist assertion, Mr. Emerson himself spoke in statements, not questions; and he would have shied away from the Christian connotation of "Kingdom of Heaven" and preferred an allusion to Hamatreya or Brahma or the Kingdom of Pan ("the patient Pan," "the eternal Pan"). Although Emily's prayer "In the name of the Bee — / And of the Butterfly — / And of the Breeze — Amen!" suggests the immanent Deity of Parker's Natural-Religious view, it is expressed in a parody of the Christian formula whose playfulness is utterly serious. Emily recognized the complicated motive: when we have lost something precious, we hasten to compensate by fashioning its image elsewhere, perhaps within ourselves, perhaps in Nature.[54]

> And a Suspicion, like a Finger
> Touches my Forehead now and then
> That I am looking oppositely
> For the site of the Kingdom of Heaven —
>
> (P 959, II.695)

Emily Dickinson could not say as wholeheartedly as Frost's protagonist in *A Masque of Mercy* (whose mother "was left over from the Brook Farm venture"): "I say I'd rather be lost in the woods / Than found in church."

Unsatisfied by Emerson's pagan paradise, she had to invest the new-found Eden through image and metaphor with the import of the Christian faith which she had rejected. So she came to speak of creative energy as an inexplicable force much like Edwards' "indwelling vital principle" of grace — in fact, precisely a "Conversion of the Mind / Like Sanctifying in the Soul." Christening by water in the country church was super-seded by a new baptism, in which the poet freely gave herself to the call of a full natural existence.[55] Thereafter natural ecstasy corresponded to God's grace, and even the impermanence of ec-stasy was transformed into the renunciation which was a sign of justification and election. The only commandment was to "Consider the Lilies" each ordained day, for Nature was the sacrament unto sanctification and spring the miracle of redemp-tion and resurrection.[56] The process of "sacramental" experience constituted, in Thoreauvian terms, the "natural Sabbath" of heaven at home:

> Some keep the Sabbath going to Church —
> I keep it, staying at Home —
>
> .   .   .   .
>
> So instead of getting to Heaven, at last —
> I'm going, all along.   (P 324, I.254–55)

Here again Emily Dickinson circles back to her point of de-parture. If she had her Sabbath in Nature, it was still in some sense a Sabbath, as it was not for Thoreau. Moreover, at the same time that the poems constructed a new Sabbath in a ro-mantic Eden, the term "old-fashioned" began to take on warm and comfortable associations. She often claimed to be old-fash-ioned; she dressed and looked old-fashioned; with another turn of the fancy she could even dress Eden up in New England garb: "Eden is that old-fashioned House"; in fact, "Nature is 'old-fashioned,' perhaps a Puritan."[57] She could not resolve the paradox (or was it a contradiction?) logically or intellectually. Its origin, if not its resolution, lay in her emotional character. By yoking together two sets of associations she attempted to reconcile metaphorically her divided consciousness.

In reality, of course, a mutable earth could not really be heaven — if there were such a place. In the imagery of the poems noon declines into twilight and dawn only follows night. She might say, "That a pansy is transitive, is its only pang. This, precluding that, is indeed divine"; but she knew that the pang was real and fatal. In the grip of ecstasy she might accept the life-process, but still she was left with the compulsion to escape a "rotatory" life and the "ceaseless flight of the seasons." [58] The transforming experience was the momentous interview — the "*separated* hour . . . more pure and true than *ordinary* hours," the "supreme italic" that punctuated life's course.[59] But, suspended between italics, she could only relive earlier bliss in memory or anticipate bliss to come:

> Looking back is best that is left
> Or if it be — before —
> Retrospection is Prospect's half,
> Sometimes, almost more.   (P 995, II.720)

Unable to rest, Emily Dickinson cast herself before and after. Prospect and retrospect became major themes in her poetry: [60] in the desperate race with time they enabled her to keep in sight the emblazoned signposts that marked the journey; they solaced her in the empty stretches that intervened.

Emily Dickinson hoped that she had discarded the Calvinist God for another Deity who was friend instead of foe, but she found that her relation to Him was in many respects unchanged. He remained the unknown Jove-Jehovah, hurling lightning-bolts and leaving a stricken "little girl" to make what she could of the experience. If He lent no abiding stay, she would have to provide of herself, and turn once again to her own creative resources. Poetry had to do more than "pile like Thunder to it's close / Then crumble grand away." [61] She would have to make its image catch and keep the blinding flash.

Emerson had already ponderously pronounced in the verses which preface the essay on "Art":

> 'Tis the privilege of Art
> Thus to play its cheerful part,
> Man in earth to acclimate
> And bend the exile to his fate,
> And, moulded of one element
> With the days and firmament,
> Teach him on these stairs to climb
> And live on even terms with Time;
> Whilst upper life the slender rill
> Of human life doth overfill.

Emily Dickinson also came, though less sanguinely, to conceive of art as the mediator between time and eternity. Isolating certain things from the flux, "We hasten to adorn" and use them, in order to construct marmoreal art; thereby "We — temples build" [62] — not public temples but private shrines for the meeting of spirit and Spiritus. As an artist she made permanent the momentary acts of consciousness despite time's inexorable wheel. She might say that she lived in an Eden of unfading seasons and perpetual noon, but such a world existed only in her saying it — that is, only in the transcendent ordering of art. Over the last century and a half, poets have come to rely increasingly on this redeeming and immortalizing function of art: Wordsworth recollected and recorded in tranquillity, and Keats aspired to the nightingale's song and the moving stillness of the urn.

Faced with the increasing difficulty of coming to terms with personal experience within the safety of received religion, Emily Dickinson like many modern poets affirmed her supreme (and religious) dedication to comprehending her experience through the intense concentration of artistic expression. For Yeats the choice between religion and art was the "perfection of the life" or the perfection "of the work." In "Vacillation" he wrote:

> I — though heart might find relief
> Did I become a Christian man and choose for my belief
> What seems most welcome in the tomb — play a predestined part.
> Homer is my example and his unchristened heart.*

For Yeats the part was not a rejection of heaven but a commitment to transmuting time's torments into "the artifice of eternity." For her own reasons Emily Dickinson rejected the comforts of Christianity and felt compelled to choose instead the life of the conscious artist. Only in conscious experience — if anywhere — could she find herself; and only in the perfection of art — if anywhere — would she escape the temporal wheel on which self turned. Born in Congregational Amherst half a century before Yeats, she could not transport herself to Byzantium any more easily than to Emerson's Eden. Still she lived for her own poetry and said to herself and to her neighbors: "Who has not found the Heaven — below — / Will fail of it above — " 63

6

In the history of the New England spirit Emily Dickinson occupies a pivotal place. Puritan orthodoxy had reached its culmination as a religious and social order in the mid-seventeenth century and a century later had found its most magnificent exponent in Jonathan Edwards, after the order itself had begun to pull apart. By the 1850's Emerson had reinvigorated the New England spirit, but only by isolating certain aspects of Edwards' thought and combining and infusing them with the vitality of

---

* Reprinted with permission of The Macmillan Co. from *Collected Poems* by William Butler Yeats (New York, 1956), p. 247. Copyright by The Macmillan Co., renewed 1961 by Bertha Georgie Yeats.

Transcendentalism. Nevertheless, by so doing Emerson brought about a further disintegration of the great Puritan synthesis, a separation of the heart from the head, just as Benjamin Franklin, Charles Chauncy, and Andrewes Norton represented a separation of the head from the heart. For all his Calvinism — or rather precisely because of his acceptance of Calvinism with his mind and heart — Edwards was a more complete person than any of these men.

Emily Dickinson points to the end of the tradition not because she represents, as Emerson does, a splintering off of part of that tradition, but because she embodies in her life and poetry the painful divisions that sundered the New England mind. Emerson was essentially a serene soul, as she was essentially a tormented one. He could be happy because out of selected fragments he had made a shining new faith — shorn now of sin and dogma and devils. To reliance on the intuitive vision of the man-god in a sinless Eden he gave thumping assent with all the eloquent enthuaism of the poet-preacher. But as Emily Dickinson realized — along with Hawthorne and Melville — he had had to close his mind and heart to much of the complex reality in order to achieve this serenity.

There is no indication that Emily Dickinson was acquainted with the writings of Jonathan Edwards; but from the remarks she made he was associated in her mind with the faith of the fathers.[64] Since what remained of New England Protestantism seemed to her intellectually preposterous and emotionally spurious, she heeded Emerson's call to the poet's rather than the Christian's vocation. With Wordsworth and Emerson and Whitman, she sought to find herself by losing herself, to lose herself by opening "an original relation to the universe." For dazzling moments she and the world were transfigured into divinity, but the difficulty lay in holding the transfiguration in a sustaining vision. In a late poem she weighed "Orpheus' Sermon" against the preacher's, or Emerson's sermon against Edwards', and aligned herself again with Emerson and the "warbling teller." [65] Nevertheless, her unshakable conception of reality and awareness of the human condition were derived not so much from Emerson as from the "old-fashioned" Puritans:

> Paradise is that old mansion
> Many owned before —
> Occupied by each an instant
> Then reversed the Door —
> Bliss is frugal of her Leases
> Adam taught her Thrift
> Bankrupt once through his excesses —
>
> (P 1119, II.787)

These seven lines of an unfinished poem rehearse all the major elements of the Puritan "vision": the initial harmony of the universe; man's violation of that harmony and his consequent alienation; the possibility of reunion and its fulfillment in visionary instants; the bankruptcy of life without vision.

In Dickinson's poetry there is a determined rigor of sight and mind which is largely lacking in Emerson: a flinty honesty which would spare her nothing, which wished (in Thoreau's words) "to live deliberately, to front only the essential facts of life," to know the abyss as well as the empyrean. There is a complexity of sensibility that brings us back to Bradford, Taylor, and Edwards and is found among the Transcendentalists perhaps only at times in Thoreau. Yet in Emily Dickinson this double consciousness finds resolution neither in Emerson's and Thoreau's belief in heaven here nor in Edwards' faith in heaven hereafter. The complexity of her mind is not the complexity of harmony but that of dissonance. Her peculiar burden was to be a Romantic poet with a Calvinist's sense of things; to know transitory ecstasy in a world tragically fallen and doomed. Her poems display a range and variety of emotional experience which far surpass that of Edwards, Emerson, Thoreau, or Whitman, but the work of all these men has a wholeness, a consistency, and finally a repose which hers lacks. She could be possessed only by the experience of the immediate moment, and so her art expressed itself in short lyrics each of which incarnated a moment. As a result her poetry emerged not in a consistent and overmastering design but in an intricate pattern of individual and contrasting fragments.

In Emily Dickinson the opposing tendencies that divided the New England mind met at cross-purposes, and after her the tendencies were to diverge again. One line of development would lead to T. S. Eliot, who was able in mid-twentieth century to hold timeless moments amid the stretching wastes of time by subsuming them both again in the Christian vision. For Eliot, perfection of the life and perfection of the work converged once more to a single center; mind and heart and art moved with one purpose; his beginning and his end were the Alpha and the Omega. That he could pursue his purpose, however, only away from his native shores signalized, in the one direction, the all-but-final collapse of the New England tradition. Of those who stayed at home, Robinson Jeffers' Calvinist sensibility could find root only in the brute beauty of the wilderness on the opposite coast. Of those who stayed in New England, Robert Frost exemplifies in many respects another line of development that proceeded from Emily Dickinson. In Frost's poetry — "Bereft," for example — man is alone in an indifferent universe without Edwards' grace or Emerson's Reason or Jeffers' pantheism; he sees "neither out far nor in deep"; from nature (no longer with a capital N) he receives either no response, as in "The Most of It," or at best an indecipherable hint that might be something or nothing, as in "For Once, Then, Something." In a chaos without objective absolutes Frost draws his materials from experience and imposes his own order in "the figure a poem makes"; perfection of the work provides "a momentary stay against confusion." [66] Robert Lowell, the most distinguished of the younger New England poets, would readily agree: obsessed by a dead tradition and a shattered world, he sought refuge in Catholicism for a time; now he sifts the pieces through his mind, constructing blazing cries of loss and failure.

In the long list of those who saw "New Englandly," Emily Dickinson occupied a critical position. She came after the fatal cleavage that split the Puritan mind between 1740 and 1840, and in her, for the last time, the dislocated elements came together to struggle for articulation, if not for readjustment, before they diverged, by Henry Adams' law of acceleration, to dissipate their last energies. The astonishing and characteristic thing about Emily Dickinson is that at the crosspoint of the X she could have written both these quatrains about earth and heaven:

> In thy long Paradise of Light
> No moment will there be
> When I shall long for Earthly Play
> And mortal Company —   (P 1145, II.803)

> God is indeed a jealous God —
> He cannot bear to see
> That we had rather not with Him
> But with each other play.   (P 1719, III.1159)

THE BUSINESS OF CIRCUMFERENCE: THE LIFE OF THE DOUBLE CONSCIOUSNESS

Emily Dickinson was sufficiently versed in country things to know that the horse that kicks free of the traces and bolts the barn seldom returns to the security of "home":

> The Life that tied too tight escapes
> Will ever after run
> With a prudential look behind
> And spectres of the Rein —
> The Horse that scents the living Grass
> And sees the Pastures smile
> Will be retaken with a shot
> If he is caught at all —   (P 1535, III.1058)

But what security did the pasture's freedom afford? Only the individual's resilience and resources. Lack of commitment to external absolutes drove the search within, pivoted the mind to turn and turn upon itself, so that the new freedom came to seem perhaps a new prison: "Captivity is Consciousness — / So's Liberty" (P384, I.304). Nevertheless, for better or for worse, the Americans of the new generation, as Emerson observed, "were born with knives in their brain, a tendency to introversion, self-dissection, anatomizing of motives." Theodore Parker proudly claimed to extract all his thinking from the "facts of conscious-ness given by the instinctive action of human nature itself." Bronson Alcott's conversations with his pupils were an explora-tory process which nudged the consciousness to perception and articulation. No matter how far or in what direction the process led, the Romantic mind began with the assertion that (in Thor-eau's words) "I only know myself as a human entity; the scene, so to speak, of thoughts and affections . . ." Knowledge was the realization of the self — ideally a complete awareness of one's thoughts and affections. Hence "the poet is he that hath fat enough, like bears and marmots, to suck his claws all winter. He hibernates in this world, and feeds on his own marrow . . ." So for Emily Dickinson the romp in the pasture's living grass was an experience that pertained to a central activity within; in fact, all experience finally mattered only as it modified the self:

> Growth of Man — like Growth of Nature —
> Gravitates within —
> Atmosphere, and Sun endorse it —
> But it stir — alone —
>
> Each — it's difficult Ideal
> Must achieve — Itself —
> Through the solitary prowess
> Of a Silent Life —
>
> Effort — is the sole condition —
> Patience of Itself —
> Patience of opposing forces —
> And intact Belief —   (P 750, II.571)

The conditions of the Silent Life, she already knew, would be demanding. First, the effort of watchful attention from instant to instant; next, the "Patience of opposing forces," whose cease-less tilt and shift were stabilized only by the steady "Patience of

Itself" — that is, by the "intact Belief" in the underlying sound-ness of consciousness. At times consciousness seemed inadequate unto itself — a "polar privacy" in which an "awful stranger" stalked the shadows. Still, the "most profound experiment / Appointed unto Men" was the consignment to the Silent Life, doubly aware as it was both "of Neighbors and the Sun" and of death. Moreover, it must be a total consignment, because "to live is so startling, it leaves but little room for other occupations."[1] The brave and redemptive act of the will was to root one's self in one's human individuality and, facing life and death, to gamble on the adventure of the mind in a world of sense.

After all, despite the multiplicity of the sensory world, " 'Tis Units — make the Swarm — "; and in a field of random impressions the self was the center of magnetic attraction and response. Self meant both uniqueness and separateness of identity: "each Mind is itself, like a distinct Bird." Since the "columnar Self" stands alone, it must stand self-sufficient, secure in

> . . . the Certainty
>
> That Lever cannot pry —
> And Wedge cannot divide
> Conviction — That Granitic Base —
>
> (P 789, II.595)

As Thoreau said, "If I am not I, who will be?" Emily told Higginson, "There is always one thing to be grateful for — that one is one's self & not somebody else." Mrs. Higginson thought the sentiment "singularly out of place in E. D.'s case," but the sole justification for her existence was the self sustained even in the knowledge of its bounds:

> She knows herself an incense small —
> Yet *small* — she sighs — if *All* — is *All* —
> How *larger* — be? (P 284, I.203)

If the self was All, it dared (in revealing metaphors) stand "alone / As a Church" and be its own "Native Land," its own New England meetinghouse. So irrevocable was its daring commitment that the self which, in Emily's words, was first "given to me by the Gods — / When I was a little Girl" could now seem "that indestructible estate." More infinite than Infinity, it would have to retain its integrity in whatever problematic afterlife there might be.[2]

In the end it was not just that the self was all one had, but that it could contain the All, be the All, displace the All:

> The Sea said "Come" to the Brook —
> The Brook said "Let me grow" —
> The Sea said "Then you will be a Sea —
> I want a Brook — Come now"!
>
> The Sea said "Go" to the Sea —
> The Sea said "I am he
> You cherished" — "Learned Waters —
> Wisdom is stale — to Me"   (P 1210, III.843)

In this dialogue between the Sea and the Brook it is the infinite Sea which importunes, eager to drink the Brook's welling power, envious and afraid of the Sea it will become. The Brook's replies hint at the might of its resources, so that after the first stanza it is no longer called a Brook and the second stanza phrases its defiance as "The Sea said 'Go' to the Sea." It could banish the engulfing absolute because it had become, in a manner of speaking, its own absolute. Like the Brook, Emily Dickinson resisted stale wisdom to cry to God and her neighbors "Let me grow" and to sing, like Whitman and Thoreau, a "Song of Myself," or, perhaps more accurately in her case, to sing "songs of myself."

There are frequent geographical images of exploration and discovery in Dickinson poems,[3] as in the Transcendentalists — for example, in the conclusion of *Walden*. But her motive for self-discovery and self-exploration was fundamentally different from that of Emerson and of most of the Transcendentalists. Emerson could call the self the "Unknown Centre"; but soon he was musing about "the world, as flowing perpetually outward from an invisible, unsounded centre in himself, centre alike of him and of them," and the next step was to dissolve it all in the euphoric perfection of the "aboriginal Self on which a universal reliance may be grounded." Although Thoreau was more wary of losing the self in the Oversoul, he could speak of "the divinity in man" and insist on the perfection of the self as self: "We hug the earth — how rarely do we mount! Methinks we might elevate ourselves a little more." Emily Dickinson could not rhapsodize about perfection or elevation so readily. Her basic motive — the highest motive that the will could command — was comprehension: to know and to feel as intensely as possible. Glorious moments would come — and she would anticipate their coming; painful moments would come — and she would dread their approach. But, in whatever guise, the moments came to *her*, and the test of the self was its decision to confront them. With this double awareness *Walden* began and Ishmael's voyage ended.

But what was the spirit which quickened the self to awareness?

> The Spirit is the Conscious Ear.*
> We actually Hear
> When We inspect — that's audible —
> That is admitted — Here —
>
> For other Services — as Sound —
> There hangs a smaller Ear
> Outside the Castle — that Contain —
> The other — only — Hear —   (P 733, II.559)

---

* Cf. Keats' lines in "Ode on a Grecian Urn":
> Heard melodies are sweet, but those unheard
>   Are sweeter; therefore, ye soft pipes, play on;
> Not to the sensual ear, but, more endeared,
>   Pipe to the spirit ditties of no tone. . .

One heard not with the ear, which caught only sound, but with what Wallace Stevens called "the delicatest ear of the mind,"[4] which made sound part of self. Experience was more than sensory; it was the individual assimilation of and response to the phenomena of sense. Emily Dickinson's conception of the soul went beyond the old categorical definitions of intellect and will, memory and reason and imagination; to her the importance of these faculties was their function in the activity through which the sensibility penetrated and absorbed and reacted to the impressions that impinged without interruption upon the individual. She heartily agreed with Emerson that

the soul in man is not an organ, but animates and exercises all the organs; is not a function, like the power of memory, of calculation, of comparison, but uses these like hands and feet; is not a faculty, but a light; is not the intellect or the will, but the master of intellect and will; is the background of our being, in which they lie. . .[5]

In other words, the soul was consciousness,[6] and consciousness was our "only home" (once again, that mighty word in the Dickinson lexicon).

While the isolate self was being constantly bombarded with impressions from without, consciousness, which was the seat of the self, was always opening out to absorb them:

> The Brain — is wider than the Sky —
> For — put them side by side —
> The one the other will contain
> With ease — and You — beside —
>
> (P 632, II.486)

In a variation on this metaphor, consciousness ("the Brain") dilated to encompass the "me" in vital association with the "not-me," projecting a circumference of greater or less diameter for which the self was the sensitive center: *

* Compare the conclusion of the chapter "The Centre of Many Circumferences" in Melville's *Mardi*: "And here, in this impenetrable retreat, centrally

> The Outer — from the Inner
> Derives it's Magnitude —
>
> .   .   .   .   .   .
>
> The fine — unvarying Axis
> That regulates the Wheel —   (P 451, I.348)

By regulating the wheeling cosmos, the circumference of the expansive consciousness became the measure of the individual self:

> Obtaining but our own Extent
> In whatsoever Realm —
> 'Twas Christ's own personal Expanse
> That bore him from the Tomb —
>
> (P 1543, III.1064)

From the outset, difficulties complicated the life of consciousness. First of all, while in one sense consciousness worked toward unity by relating the me and the not-me, in another sense it worked toward a division within the self; for while consciousness was the seat of selfhood, it had simultaneously to be somehow independent of the self, and open to everything else. "However intense my experience," said Thoreau, "I am conscious of the presence and criticism of a part of me, which, as it were, is not a part of me, but spectator, sharing no experience, but taking note of it; and that is no more I than it is you." In "Song of Myself" Whitman wrote:

> Apart from the pulling and hauling stands what I am,
> Stands amused, complacent, compassionating, idle,
>   unitary,
> Looks down, is erect, or bends an arm on an impal-
>   pable certain rest,

---

slumbered the universe-rounded, zodiac-belted, horizon-zoned, sea-girt, reef-sashed, mountain-locked, arbour-nested, royalty-girdled, arm-clasped, self-hugged, indivisible Donjalolo, absolute monarch of Juam: — the husk-inhusked meat in a nut; the innermost spark in a ruby; the juice-nested seed in a golden-rinded orange; the red royal stone in an effeminate peach; the insphered sphere of spheres."

> Looking with side-curved head curious what will
>   come next,
> Both in and out of the game and watching and
>   wondering at it.

Emily Dickinson too experienced the disquieting sense that as she knit herself to the cosmos and the cosmos to herself, she also stood aside as witness and recorder of action and response. In her quatrain quoted above, the "Brain" held in its circuit both the sky and the individual; or — to say the same thing in the image of another poem — she and consciousness were "mutual Monarch" of the self. And mutual Monarch meant dual Monarchs:

> But since Myself — assault Me —
> How have I peace
> Except by subjugating
> Consciousness?
>
> And since We're mutual Monarch
> How this be
> Except by Abdication —
> Me — of Me?   (P 642, II.494)

If there were no escape, would consciousness become a cell imprisoning the active and the passive self?

To complicate matters further, the divided consciousness faces the multiplicity of experience. W. H. Auden has stated the problem succinctly:

When I observe myself, the *I* which observes is unique, but not individual, since it has no characteristics of its own; it has only the power to recognize, compare, judge and choose: the self which it observes is not a unique identity but a succession of various states of feeling or desire.[7]

If consciousness is the only constant, then instantaneous impressions become, in Emerson's words, "a train of moods like a string of beads, and as we pass through them they prove to be many-colored lenses which paint the world their own hue, and each shows only what lies in its focus." Consequently, Emerson continued, "in this kingdom of illusions we grope eagerly for stays and foundations" and "the only ballast I know is a respect to the present hour." Thoreau agreed that the self and the universe culminated in each moment: "In any weather, at any hour of the day or night, I have been anxious to improve the nick of time, and notch it on my stick too; to stand on the meeting of two eternities, the past and the future, which is precisely the present moment; to toe that line." Emily Dickinson was urgently aware that in the life of consciousness the primary duty was to catch the irrecoverable moment.[8]

The extension of this principle turned the universe into a pageant for the individual sensibility, and the frequent theatrical images and references in the poems and letters[9] underscore her notion of the world as "this mighty show" performed every moment for her. Hence the large number of poems which set forth fresh and distinctive impressions from nature. But even these "objective" or "descriptive" poems do not merely record the sights and sounds of Nature's pageantry; these "nicks of time" are notched on her sensibility and they record as well the interaction of perception and response. That pattern includes the metaphorical associations which arose in the poet's effort at comprehension, each of which in turn involves a pattern of response — so that the assimilating of the sensory impression ends in the describing of a complex inner state which is the exact reflection of the unique experience. Often the poetic process worked back in the other direction, with consciousness prescribing as its immediate object the "definition" of its internal state. Inevitably, the poet could objectify her emotions only by embodying them in sensory images and metaphors. And so consciousness defined the inner world in terms of the outer and the outer world in terms of the inner, its arc sweeping variously around the central self.

The process of self-realization exerted an almost unbearable pressure on "a Moment's shallow Rim," [10] and the very operation of the consciousness displayed its limitations. Consciousness could never flag on its treadmill of experience; as Samuel Johnson knew, the imagination always hungered for more. But despite the intention to live each moment fully, one could not. The total comprehension of the moment meant dwelling on it while other moments fled unnoticed by. The poet might reply, quite rightly, that only certain experiences merited such lingering attention. Even so, one found one's self living not just in the present but in the past and even in the future; a life dedicated to apprehending the immediate intensity became alarmingly caught up in retrospection and anticipation.

St. Augustine had worried about the necessity of measuring "present time, when present time has no duration" in the flickering point between past and future. "It can only be that the mind . . . performs three functions, those of expectation, perception and memory" (*Confessions*, XI: 21, 28). Outside the Christian context Frost stated in "Carpe Diem": *

> But bid life seize the present?
> It lives less in the present
> Than in the future always,
> And less in both together
> Than in the past. The present
> Is too much for the senses,
> Too crowding, too confusing,
> Too present to imagine.

For Frost and Dickinson the writing itself became not just an act of comprehension but one of preservation which enabled the poet to trace the "Moment's shallow Rim" in an indelible cir-

* From *Complete Poems of Robert Frost* (New York, 1949), p. 448. Copyright 1916, 1921, 1923 by Holt, Rinehart and Winston, Inc. Copyright 1942, 1944, 1951 by Robert Frost. Reprinted by permission of Holt, Rinehart and Winston, Inc.

cumference. So Emily Dickinson wrote of the pageant of experience which paraded before her to be recorded as art:

> My Splendors, are Menagerie —
> But their Competeless Show
> Will entertain the Centuries
> When I, am long ago,
> An Island in dishonored Grass —
> Whom none but Daisies, know. (P 290, I.209)

Paradoxically, poems such as Emily Dickinson wrote transcended the present by fastening upon it, and fastened upon the present in order to transcend it. The sharp focus did, in a certain sense, fix the flux.

2

From the beginning Emily Dickinson was aware that life was "Half a transport — half a trouble" — contrary states which had somehow to be reconciled or accommodated. The poems worry again and again about the duality of experience: pain and pleasure; woe and bliss; "bandaged moments" and "moments of Escape"; moments of impotence and "Moments of Dominion"; hell and heaven; torment and grace.[11] Consciousness was divided not only in its internal function but in its apprehension of objective reality.

At times she could convince herself that it was her voluntary renunciation and abstinence which earned the purer moments of transport.[12] More frequently she had to regard loss and death as the spurs whose pain made joy more vital.

> To Those who know
> The Stimulus there is
> In Danger — Other impetus
> Is numb — and Vitalless —   (P770, II.584)

In other words, "We buy with Contrast"; in a kind of "compensation" we "learn the Transport by the Pain — / As Blind Men learn the Sun!" That pleasure was distilled from pain, that blindness strained for vision — the force of these truths kept the wheel spinning. Time and death were lost in transport, and this brief liberation made time and death more mocking than before. Among the papers found in Emily Dickinson's drawer after her death was a scrap which read simply: "A woe of Ecstasy." [13]

Emerson had taken cognizance of the "inevitable dualism" which "bisects nature," so that "one prevails now, all buzz and din; and the other prevails then, all infinitude and paradise . . ." But this "dualism" was easily explained in terms of the levels of human perception; man is conscious of "two lives, of the understanding and of the soul," of temporal transactions and "flash-of-lightning faith." For Emerson, man's emergence into godhead was always balked by the "backstroke," the "kick of the gun," which kept him merely human. Still, the law of compensation did not tear Nature apart, but stabilized it in the harmonious Unity which is its source. The seeming limitations of Fate and contradictions of Design were rightly understood not as inherent defects but as challenges which the individual could combat in his gradual progress toward the Unity-Trinity of Truth, Beauty, and Goodness.

Emerson's sense of the double consciousness was radically different from that of Emily Dickinson. Emerson's world was, first and last, animated by the moral sense: "Thus is the universe alive. All things are moral." Perception resulted in right behavior, and Beauty was really considered only as it pertained to the conduct of life. Nothing could be further from the concerns of Emily Dickinson. Her mind was oblivious to the ethical preoccupations of Emerson and of the Thoreau who could write: "Our whole life is startlingly moral. There is never an instant's truce between virtue and vice." Her only standards of judgment were those of the Thoreau whose "*purely* senuous life" was regulated not by understanding and reason, nor by virtue and vice, but by pleasure and pain.

It is the aspiration to the *"purely* sensuous life" of the poetic consciousness that makes the initially improbable bond between two provincial New Englanders like Thoreau and Dickinson and John Keats, who had exclaimed: "O for a life of Sensations rather than of Thoughts." The words "sensuous" and "sensations" have a particular meaning in this context. Far from drifting toward hedonism, these three poets made the commitment to "sensations" the basis of their moral and poetic life. Dissatisfied with philosophical and theological explanations of existence and distrustful of the speculation of intellect, they concentrated upon their concrete and immediate experience. Dickinson listed Keats among her special poets,[14] for Keats had known that consciousness moved between pleasure and pain. Melancholy, he wrote,

> dwells with Beauty — Beauty that must die;
>   And Joy, whose hand is ever at his lips
> Bidding adieu; and aching Pleasure nigh,
>   Turning to poison while the bee-mouth sips:
> Ay, in the very temple of Delight
>   Veil'd Melancholy has her sovran shrine,
>   Though seen of none save him whose strenuous tongue
> Can burst Joy's grape against his palate fine;
>   His soul shall taste the sadness of her might,
>   And be among her cloudy trophies hung.

In this "vale of Soul-making" a poet defined his identity by living out the pleasure and the pain and by telling that truth in art. Keats formulated his creed as "Beauty is truth, truth beauty, — that is all / Ye know on earth, and all ye need to know." * Emily Dickinson added:

---

* Emerson could write, "The true philosopher and the true poet are one, and a truth, which is beauty, is the arm of both" (*Nature, Addresses, and Lectures*, p. 59). However, truth was important to the philosopher and beauty

> I died for Beauty — but was scarce
> Adjusted in the Tomb
> When One who died for Truth, was lain
> In an adjoining Room —
>
> He questioned softly "Why I failed"?
> "For Beauty", I replied —
> "And I — for Truth — Themself are One —
> We Bretheren, are", He said —   (P 449, I.347)

For neither poet was Truth an ethical imperative but rather a vision of reality, and both Keats and Dickinson were more consistently "amoral" (in this sense) than was Thoreau.*

From beginning to end, however, Emily Dickinson remained a deep-dyed New Englander, and Jonathan Edwards is perhaps the writer whose temper and Augustinian sense of "compensation" most closely resemble hers. In the *Confessions* (*VIII*, 3) St. Augustine spoke of the "ebb and flow" of joy and pain as the "rhythm of our world": "it is always the case that the greater the joy, the greater is the pain which precedes it." In his meditations Edwards wrote:

. . . it is ordered that so many of our outward mercies and good things are given in a way of deliverance, protection, or remedy from some calamity we have been the subjects of or exposed to. Thus God rather gives us clothing to cover our nakedness than to make us without any deformity and nakedness we should be ashamed of.

But man's acceptance of the deformity of things revealed in compensation such "positive blessedness and glory" in creation that

almost all men, and those that seem to be very miserable, love life,

---

to the poet as they influenced the right conduct of life. Neither Keats nor Dickinson would add goodness to truth and beauty.

* Cf. Wallace Stevens' remark: "The morality of the poet's radiant and productive atmosphere is the morality of the right sensation" (*The Necessary Angel*, London: Faber & Faber, 1960, p. 58).

because they cannot bear to lose sight of such a beautiful and lovely world. The ideas, that every moment whilst we live have a beauty that we take not distinct notice of, brings a pleasure that, when we come to the trial, we had rather live in much pain and misery than lose.[15]

Without sharing his theological and ethical assumptions, Emily would have known exactly what Edwards meant; although she accepted many of Emerson's ideas, she responded with Edwards' sensibility. How much more reminiscent of Edwards than of Emerson is this poem of "compensation":

> Must be a Wo —
> A loss or so —
> To bend the eye
> Best Beauty's way —
>
> .   .   .   .   .   .
>
> A Common Bliss
> Were had for less —
> The price — is
> Even as the Grace —
>
> Our lord — thought no
> Extravagance
> To pay — a Cross —   (P 571, II.436)

On the other hand, while Edwards' sensibility functioned within the Christian context, Emily Dickinson, like Emerson, or more especially Thoreau, made the cultivation of consciousness her religion. The climactic stanza of the poem above makes the point explicit: the individual's experience is religious experience, like Christ's pain and bliss; religion and consciousness are one and the same. In a similar correlation between Spirit and spirit Frost reversed the order and concluded that the Incarnation is not really "God's own descent / Into flesh" but rather the soul's activity in the body:

> one mighty charge
> On our human part
> Of the soul's ethereal
> Into the material.[16]

3

In a body of poetry devoted to the main concerns of consciousness the principal themes are, predictably, love, death, and immortality: fulfillment, dissolution, and transcendence inextricably entwined. The need for love — that is, for external union which would complete and express the self — is the force that pervades all of Emily Dickinson's writing: "My love for those I love — not many — not very many, but dont I love them so?"; " 'Little children, love one another.' Not all of life to live, is it, nor all of death to die"; "That Love is all there is,/ Is all we know of Love"; "For just one Plaudit famishing,/ The Might of human love." Of such sacred importance is love that it is church, sacrament, grace.[17]

Nevertheless, when Austin Dickinson filed Emily's death certificate, he answered the question asking "Sex, and whether single, Married, or Widowed" not by the obvious entry "Female, single," but by the curious statement, *never married*,"[18] which emphasizes for us not so much the clarity as the ambiguity of her situation. The lady who thought that "Love is all there is" shunned not only marriage but almost any association outside of the sheltering family roof. Her own words state her ambivalence: "We dare not touch [Human Affection], yet flee, what else remains?" Even in heaven she would have the same difficulty: "I fear we shall care very little for the technical resurrection, when to behold the one face that to us comprised it is too much for us, and I dare not think of the voraciousness of that only gaze and its only return."[19]

How could she love and not submit to the voraciousness of love? First, by careful and rigorous selection, which she would call "election." The privilege which set her apart from others was "the White Election"; it allowed her to "Choose One" as the object of her devotion, "Then — close the valves of her attention — / Like Stone." The next step of exclusion, which would finally eliminate even the lover, was the supposition that the "incidents of love / Are more than it's Events" [20] — that external relationships mean less than internal feelings. The initial object of her love mattered little to the experience of love. By choice and by exclusion love existed only within — and hence, in a sense, only with — herself; her "lover" existed in the craving of her nature, and was allowed to exist only as the figment (or should one say fiction?) of her imagination.

Among the many poems about love [21] there is one (P 196, I.141) which exemplifies the convolutions of her emotional character. It is about the love shared by the poet and someone whom she calls Tim, and the refrain is "Tim and I." At the beginning of the poem Tim is clearly the unspecified man elected for intimate association, and so "we bolt the door tight / To prevent a friend." Undeluded by dreams, they "see to the end" of life: they are in love but must die. "Tim — reads a little Hymn" — like a good clergyman (Wadsworth?) — and "we both pray" to die simultaneously. "How shall we arrange" such a remarkable coincidence, the poet asks; but scattered clues have already anticipated the last line. The poet has so consistently used a combination of singular and plural references ("our brave face," "our hand," "our brown eye") that the reader has begun to suspect that the association between "Tim and I" is closer than at first supposed. Indeed it is closer — and different — as the last line rephrases the refrain to make their identification explicit: "I — 'Tim' — and — Me!" Wooing her "lover" in the privacy of her mind, she might well place them, as she did in another poem (P1548, III.1068), among the great lovers and more particularly among the romantic star-crossed lovers of history.

It would be presumptuous and pointless to claim that if Emily had had a husband or a lover, her yearning would have been fulfilled. She assured herself — and she was almost certainly right — that human love would never have been enough:

> I could suffice for Him, I knew —
> He — could suffice for Me —
> Yet Hesitating Fractions — Both
> Surveyed Infinity —   (P 643, II.495)

"Would I be Whole" joined with just a person? The answer "No" left one "face to face with Nature" and "with God." The need for union extended beyond passion and possibility to a craving for universal love, for all life and all being.

Consequently, on all levels — human, sexual, religious, and mystical — Emily Dickinson's love was doomed, by its very nature and demands, to retire to itself in unrequited frustration. Her imagination then embodied her frustration in the "lover" whom she prided herself for having denied:

> I cannot live with You —
> It would be Life —
> And Life is over there —   (P 640, II.492)

If she could not admit to a lover in life either within her mind or outside of it, then the lover would associate himself with the prospect of death, and from the beginning she could not distinguish love from loss, pain, and finally death.[22] Since there was no hope, she could only draw what satisfaction she could from hopelessness. So the poetic metamorphosis of the "lover" from Wadsworth, the minister of the Calvary Church, to the "Man of Sorrows" (Wadsworth's image in her imagination) to Christ Himself was a transformation which, by conscious intent or not, served to glorify her in her convulsions of pain. She was not an ordinary woman wailing her lost love; she was "Queen of Calvary," "Empress of Calvary." Agony held its own exaltation, its own catharsis, its own canonization, and in triumphant agony she invoked metaphors of Calvary, crucifixion, and martyrdom for the experience of love.[23] Lovers were "Ordained to Suffering"; they moved "through Calvaries of Love"; "Each bound the Other's Crucifix." In her mind and in her poems, love, death, and religious sacrifice were so confused that death became the erotic apotheosis which vindicated a doomed life — an eroticism permissible now to the Puritan, and even holy precisely because it was painful.

The dwelling on death for a morbidly sentimental thrill was particularly popular among writers and readers of the nineteenth century. Even more than Dickens and Irving and Mrs. Stowe, less durable writers such as N. P. Willis, Donald Grant Mitchell, and Lydia Sigourney, the "Sweet Singer of Hartford," specialized in exploring all the possibilities of the theme of love and death, and they were rewarded for their tears by a large and damp-eyed audience, who read them avidly in books, magazines, and gift annuals. Given her temperament and situation, Emily Dickinson could not but be affected by this mortuary writing: * she clipped from the newspaper a lugubrious poem entitled "The Life-Clock" and on another occasion an advertisement for tombstones; she shivered to the words of Harriet Prescott Spofford; she copied out the "sweet" verses of Reverend John Pierpont to send on the third anniversary of a friend's sister's death.[24] There are poems of Dickinson which almost suggest Huckleberry Finn's description of Emmeline Grangerford's macabre fancy and others whose necrophilic preoccupation outdoes everybody except perhaps Poe. The poet dies again and again; she is laid out in the coffin; she bends over to catch her lover's dying breath; she looks forward to fondling his corpse and preparing him for burial; she

---

* How different from all this, how much less sentimental (and, in a way, how much colder) is Thoreau's strenuous effort to view "the phenomenon of death" as part of the life cycle in which the individual's chief concern should be, "How may a man most cleanly and gracefully get out of nature?"

anticipates love in a shared grave.[25] Fortunately, even the worst of Emily Dickinson's poems about death [26] so far exceed the limits of Mrs. Sigourney's sensibility and skill that there is no need to press the point longer; nor can this morbidity be ascribed completely to popular taste.

In the pattern of her mind, since "The Test of Love — is Death," then death itself came as a lover; since death was crowned with power, he came as a lover-king; since death justified the "Guilt" of love, he came as a lover-redeemer.[27] Dying itself was merely the passage, often depicted as a carriage ride, to love, coronation, heaven:

> Because I could not stop for Death —
> He kindly stopped for me —
> The Carriage held but just Ourselves —
> And Immortality.   (P 712, II.546)

In several poems it is impossible to identify the "him" as lover, death, or Christ; one (P1123, II.788–89) speaks of the "tender Carpenter" nailing the coffin down — and that suggests the lover or death — but the variant speaks of the "sovereign Carpenter" — and that suggests death or Christ. The significant fact is that Emily Dickinson did not make the distinction in her own mind.

Therefore, the final and universal lover was, as in Whitman's poetry (and in the very same epithet), "democratic Death": "The Beggar and his Queen / Propitiate this Democrat." However, although "Death's large — Democratic fingers / Rub away the Brand" of "Color — Caste — Denomination — " it was not enough for her, as it was for Whitman, that death be merely the mysterious leveler. On the contrary, death's regal "Power" conferred the "One dignity" which "delays for all." So each and all received his mighty title and estate; the brides of death were democrat-queens; the kingdom of death was an egalitarian Empire of Czars as small as Everyman.[28]

Where, then, does love become life? Only after the pain —
"over there." "Till Death — is narrow Loving —" but then "Love
is immortality." No wonder that immortality is "the Flood subject." When she and the lover had bound each other to the cross,
the figure of the man blurred with that of Christ,* and as she
shared in the exquisite agony of His love, so she would share in
His resurrection as well. Out of danger in the Eden-Heaven, all
the emotional and religious frustrations which she had endured
at such expense would be lost in her fulfillment in and absorption by the "lover"; for "years of troth have taught thee/ More
than Wifehood ever may!" Sometimes heaven ("Old Suitor
Heaven") meant an eternity wed to God, the "distant — stately
Lover." Then she would be "Bride of the Father and the Son /
Bride of the Holy Ghost": "What omnipotence lies in wait / For
her to be a Bride." Sometimes Jesus was, explicitly or implicitly,
the courtly gentleman, the Redeemer who became her Master;
at other times she rejected Jesus for her "lover" and looked forward to an immortality of "you and me" in Paradise.[29] The
identity of the heavenly "lover" — God, man, or God-man — was
often indeterminate, a shape projected by the need of the isolate
self.[30]

To Emily Dickinson, then, love is the force which drives the
cycle of life, death, and resurrection. It is "anterior to Life — /
Posterior to Death"; it is immortality, where the pangs of love
are consummated "in ravished Holiness" with an "Anguish
grander than Delight," a "Transport wild as thrills the Graves."[31]
But what could the prospect of fulfillment in the afterlife mean
to one who was alternately skeptical or fearful of immortality?
She found herself trapped in the coils of her own doubts. In one
poem, cited earlier, she writes: "I cannot live with You
. . . I could not die with You . . . Nor could I rise — with

* After Wadsworth's death Emily specifically linked Wadsworth suffering,
death, and resurrection with Christ's: L III 745.

You." The poem ends with "that White Sustenance — Despair." But if immortality in its orthodox sense led to despair, there was perhaps hope in another meaning of that word. In several places Emily linked immortality with consciousness and with moments of illumination,[32] and the association is revealing. Her only certainty of immortality was in the experience of a "moment of Deathlessness," and immortality had its deepest meaning for her, as did love and death, as an existential state of mind and feeling. To fill the void of "Missing All," consciousness could supply only itself, but within that arena (since it was the only certainty and so a kind of absolute) she could have the complete experience: love in its pain and exaltation; death in its extinction and distinction; immortality in its individuality and absorption of individuality. All this, in that closed circle — alone but safe, safe but still alone.

4

As love moved between death and immortality, as consciousness moved between woe and bliss, the poetic imagination embodied the extremes of experience in contrapuntal themes: the bird, especially the humble wren, who yet can dominate the universe with melody; the jewel, pearl, or treasure, lost, sought, and found; the homely caterpillar whose "dim capacity for Wings" becomes the butterfly bursting from the protective cocoon; "freckled human Nature" and "the freckled maiden" on the one hand and the spotlessness of her own "White Election" on the other; * the transition from want to plenty, from beggary to power, and back again; the contrast between the towering mountain and the daisy ** cringing at its foot.[33]

* A check of the associations of the color "white," as indicated by the references in the footnote, link "white" with matrimony, death, winter, the lily, the individual consciousness, the soul, God, despair, heaven. So, for Emily, as for Melville and for Poe, whiteness itself expressed or veiled the final and ambiguous mystery.

** "Daisy" was the name Emily used for herself in the letters to the "Master."

The most richly embroidered tapestry of images is worked out in a fairy-tale Arcadia of feudal chivalry,[34] of jousts and courts, of peasants, knights, and kings — where Snow White or Cinderella or Sleeping Beauty might find Prince Charming, where a little seamstress or freckled gypsy or lowly peasant might become queen. She composed poem after poem in which the condescension of the king elevates her to the power and position of the crown[35]; whereupon "She felt herself *supremer —/ A Raised — Etherial Thing!*"

> He put the Belt around my life —
> I heard the Buckle snap —
> And turned away, imperial,
> My Lifetime folding up —
> Deliberate, as a Duke would do
> A Kingdom's Title Deed —
> Henceforth, a Dedicated sort —
> A Member of the Cloud.   (P 273, I.194)

As for her:

> She rose to His Requirement — dropt
> The Playthings of Her Life
> To take the honorable Work
> Of Woman, and of Wife —   (P 732, II.558)

She celebrated her new status in several "wife" poems: [36]

> I'm "wife" — I've finished that —
> That other state —
> I'm Czar — I'm "Woman" now —
> It's safer so —
>
> .   .   .   .
>
> This being comfort — then
> That other kind — was pain —
> But why compare?
> I'm "Wife"! Stop there!   (P 199, I.142–43)

Despite her claim, Miss Dickinson would never finish with "that other state." In her seclusion from outsiders, chastity was not a physical fact but a state of mind; the virgin withheld her-self from emotional and spiritual involvement. In any relation-ship she would have to risk, and finally surrender, the autonomy of the self. She would allow the demands of love in her mind and in her poems, but even there she would not submit without a struggle, or at least a show of struggle.

She would have to be the raped virgin, a role that would permit her to be ravished but uncommitted. So she asked archly:

> Did the Harebell loose her girdle
> To the lover Bee
> Would the Bee the Harebell *hallow*
> Much as formerly?
>
> Did the "Paradise" — persuaded —
> Yield her moat of pearl —
> Would the Eden *be* an Eden,
> Or the Earl — an *Earl?*   (P 213, I.149)

The point is not that the harebell wishes to banish the "lover Bee" but rather that her hallowed purity (again it is not a ques-tion of morals but of relationships) requires that she resist and not entice the expected advances of the Earl of Eden. Elsewhere she wrote:

> Struck, was I, nor yet by Lightning —
>
> .   .   .   .
>
> Maimed — was I — yet not by Venture —
>
> .   .   .   .
>
> Robbed — was I — intact to Bandit —
> All my Mansion torn —
> Sun — withdrawn to Recognition —
> Furthest shining — done —
>
> .   .   .   .
>
> Most — I love the Cause that slew Me.
> Often as I die
> It's beloved Recognition
> Holds a Sun on Me —   (P 925, II.675–76)

The brutal violation, done in the dark with the sun withdrawn, blazes its own spectacular light, and for the sake of the Sun held on her she cherishes the ravishment above her intact virginity. The bright crash of the lightningbolt frequently symbolizes in the poetry a "rape" by Nature or by God.

Emily Dickinson found even more enticing a variation on the role of the ravished virgin — the unspoiled bride. Keats had used the phrase "still unravished bride" to characterize the inviolability of the urn as a work of art; but the poem itself associates these same paradoxical qualities with human emotion as it can be expressed within the limits of art. There — but not in the living act — one can have the passion without the exhaustion, the commitment without the consummation. The pattern is repeated in the language and imagery of the Dickinson "bride" poems: [37] "Half Child — Half Heroine"; the titled but unwritten book; the only half-conscious Queen "Royal — all but the Crown"; "The Wife — without the Sign." And so

> A solemn thing — it was — I said —
> A Woman — white — to be —
> And wear — if God should count me fit —
> Her blameless mystery —   (P 271, I.193)

Bowles referred to Emily as "the Queen Recluse," royal but remote,[38] and through all her years of seclusions she went in white, playing for her own satisfaction the chaste and mysterious bride.

In fact, her feelings were even more uncertain about the "lover" who would elevate and complete her existence:

> He was weak, and I was strong — then —
> So He let me lead him in —
> I was weak, and He was strong then —
> So I let him lead me — Home.   (P 190, I.137)

She would not always be dependent on her "Master"; he had, sometimes at least, to lean on her strong mind and heart. In some of the "wife" poems she begins by gratefully proclaiming her status as Queen-Wife but goes on to boast that although "I gave myself to Him," she also "took Himself, for Pay" and so assimilated the "Emperor of Men" into herself. As for the mighty mountain and the lowly daisy, "which, Sir, are you and which am I/ Upon an August day?" For "the tiniest ones are mightiest — The Wren will prevail." [39] She could see herself heroically waxing as Prince Charming waned:

> I rose — because He sank —
>
> . . . .
>
> I cheered my fainting Prince —
> I sang firm — even — Chants —
>
> . . . .
>
> I told him Best — must pass
> Through this low Arch of Flesh —
>
> . . . .
>
> I told him Worlds I knew
> Where Emperors grew — (P 616, II.473–74)

Then, having packed the Prince off to a distant imperial heaven, her spirit was free to mount the throne both as "Emperor" and "Sovreign — of Itself" and as "Sovreign of them all." [40] In her unmistakably feminine manner she insisted upon her inclination toward the "masculine" role throughout the poetry, so that in a sense the wedding of the beggar-maid to the King was consummated in her displacing him. The imagery of the poetry accurately projects the pattern of her consciousness. Aware of her incompleteness, yet wary of external commitments, she persisted in the effort to arrogate to herself as much of the burden, the responsibility, and the glory of experience as she could.

5

The crowning glory of those "Superior instants" came, in Emerson's phrase, with "that redundancy or excess of life which in conscious beings we call *ecstasy*." "This ecstatical state," he went on to say, "seems to direct a regard to the whole and not to the parts; to the cause and not to the end . . . It respects genius and not talent; hope, and not possession; . . . art and not works of art; poetry and not experiment . . ." Indeed, Emerson concluded, "Life is an ecstasy." With a more complex sense of things, Thoreau too exulted, "Surely joy is the condition of life," and Emily joined the paean: "I find ecstasy in living — the mere sense of living is joy enough"; "Oh Matchless Earth — We underrate the chance to dwell in Thee." [41]

Her most frequent metaphor for ecstasy was Circumference. Each of the negotiations which consciousness conducted between the me and the not-me established a circumference, but Circumference in this exalted sense carried special connotations. The circle had long been a symbol for the spirit in activity, but with great, almost contradictory, differences in its significance through the centuries. Jonathan Edwards, an eighteenth-century New England Christian, reasoned that as the universe of heavenly bodies operated in a system of wheels within wheels, and as the earth shaped its natural cycles in circular courses, "so it is in the course of things in God's providence over the intelligent and moral world, all is the motion of wheels." On all orders of existence creation was the sublime machine, and in the grand scheme of Newtonian physics the rotation of a given wheel mattered only as it contributed to the intricate design of the orderly whole. For Edwards, as "the wheels of a WATCH or a CLOCK move contrary one to another . . . yet all serve the intent of the workman to shew the time," so by extension the workings of God's creation in the moral order and the spiritual life "center in the purpose of God the great creator of all things." The central purpose was cosmic in dimension and controlled the turning of the individual wheels. In all these spheres of activity a careful distinction had to be maintained: "There is a progress towards a certain fixed issue of things, and every revolution brings nearer to that issue, as it is in the motion of a wheel upon the earth or in the motion of the wheels of a chariot, and not like the motion of a wheel on its axis, for if so, its motion would be vain . . ." [42] In spirit as in matter each wheel revolved toward its appointed end. Emerson agreed with the premise that "Unit and Universe are round," but for him, instead of functioning in the absolute plan of the cosmic clockworks, each man rather made the universe bend to coherent shape around himself, so that in Edwards' terms he made the wheel turn vainly on itself. Not at all in vain, Emerson and Thoreau insisted repeatedly, because the soul did expand from the turning center to orient the cosmos to itself: "This is the key to the power of the greatest men, — their spirit diffuses itself. A new quality travels by night and by day, in concentric circles from its origin . . ."; "We should not walk on tiptoe, but healthily expand to our full circumference on the soles of our feet." In this metaphor "the eye is the first circle; the horizon which it forms is the second; and throughout nature this primary figure is repeated without end . . . Our life is an apprenticeship to the truth that around every circle another can be drawn . . ." [43]

Emily Dickinson was at first fearful lest the "minute Circumference/ Of a single Brain" be engrossed in its "Finity," but she soon learned in the moment of ecstasy that she was "the Vital Axle" for a wheeling cosmos. There are numerous poems about the airy dilation of the expansive consciousness [44] as it "Went out upon Circumference —/ Beyond the Dip of Bell." She was never to lose completely the sense of her insignificance; the poems keep coming back to the paradox of her bigness and her diminutiveness. However, at moments the smallest event — like the grain of sand which comprehended all things, like Walden Pond which mingled the waters of the world, like Whitman's gathering on the Brooklyn Ferry — could sustain in a miraculous sphere the furthest reaches of space and the fullness of human existence: "Behold how great a firmament/ Accompanies a Star"; "Existence's whole Arc, filled up,/ With one small Diadem."

At the same time that the universe was gravitating to the individual center, the individual was gravitating to an absolute center, groping toward it as it was perceived in intuitive flashes. For this reason, Emerson said, Nature must be considered "the organ through which the universal spirit speaks to the individual, and strives to lead back the individual to it"; and for this reason Thoreau once drew the figure of his mind not as a circle but as a parabola or "non-returning curve" opening out westward. Emily, too, felt instinctively that whether "Expressed — or still — " there "exists in every Human Nature/ A Goal," so that "each life converges" in its Circumference to some further center.[45]

Emerson had noted that "St. Augustine described the nature of God as a circle whose centre was everywhere and its circumference nowhere," and Emily imagined eternity as a state which was "Circumference without Relief —/ Or Estimate — or End" and "Centre, there, all the time."[46] Both were saying that a true circle is a phenomenon of time and space which has (from the individual's viewpoint) "God, for a frontier." So in several poems Circumference marked the line between "Place" and "Presence," between "Firmament below" and "Firmament above."[47] Circumference represented the farthest boundary of human experience, where two modes of being touched, where that which was circle pressed that which was beyond. At the same time, Circumference also marked the "terminus" of human delimitation.[48] The doubleness of the metaphor — extension and limit — makes an important point, for in Dickinson, as in Emerson and Thoreau, eternity and infinity and God Himself can best be taken as the encircling infinity into which the individual may expand in accordance with his inner capacity.* In its various contexts and multiple associations Circumference comes to serve as a complex symbol for those disrupted moments when in some sense time transcends time. Circumference signifies ecstasy in its expansiveness, in its self-contained wholeness, in its self-ordered coherence, in its definition of the individual's capacity for being (and for Being). For the duration of the ecstasy, at least, man seems a "Finite Infinity," and God's "larger Glory" seems "for the less / A just sufficient Ring." [49]

Conversely, Circumference acts too as an indispensable defense perimeter which separates man from God and "secures Eternity/ From presenting — Here." [50] Edwards believed that ecstasy was possible for man only through God-given concentricity with Himself; for he believed with St. Augustine that personality found its reference point not in an impersonal All-Center, which was Emerson's vague absolute, but in the very Person of the Deity. Emily Dickinson found her God incomprehensible as a Person; He was faceless, indeterminate — and hence menacing. Exposure threatened the integrity and identity of the individual by opening him to obliteration by the Absolute, to engulfment by anonymous Being. In self-defense Emily Dickinson came to see Circumference not simply as the limits of possibility but as the positive protection against "Mortal Abolition." As far as she could tell, she could only be Emily Dickinson within the circle of "that revolving reason/ Whose esoteric belt/ Protects our sanity" from blank and inhuman Infinitude,

* See also Frost's lines:

> Though our leap in air
> Prove as vain a hop
> As the hop from grass
> Of a grasshopper,
> Don't discount our powers;
> We have made a pass
> At the infinite . . .

From *In the Clearing* (New York, 1962), p. 54. Copyright © 1956, 1962 by Robert Frost. Reprinted by permission of Holt, Rinehart and Winston, Inc.

"Whose Amplitude no end invades — / Whose Axis never comes." [51]

In the complexity of its operation Circumference could perform the complementary functions of extension and enclosure, of release from self and determination of self. Moreover, Circumference's "Processes of Size" ended in cessation of movement, which fixed, for the instant anyway, its own limits: "When Cogs — stop — that's Circumference — / The Ultimate — of Wheels." [52] The poetry employs related images for Circumference: the crown, the pearl, the horizon, the disc, the arc of the bird's flight, the sheen of the noon sun. [53] In most cases there is the same connotation of bounded breadth, of concrete dimension: "For sheen must have a disk/ To be a sun," just as consciousness must have a body to be a person.

The word which Emily Dickinson summoned most frequently to suggest her response to Circumferential experience was "Awe." [54] The associations of Awe tied together a knot of qualities and dispositions for which the more common word in the eighteenth and nineteenth centuries was the "sublime," and thereby, whether she realized it or not, she placed herself in the Romantic cult of the sublime. The landscape images which she grouped in various poems around the concept of Awe make a magnificent panoramic prospect: clouded sunset; misty mountains; starlit night; midnight; lightning; volcano; fire; earthquake; towering heights; surging sea; polar ice floes. [55] Not only do these images call to mind the landscapes of Washington Allston, Thomas Cole, and the "Hudson River School," but they bear astonishing resemblance to the list of natural phenomena which Kant had compiled in *Critique of Judgement* to exemplify the sublime:

Bold, overhanging, and as it were threatening, rocks; clouds piled up in the sky, moving with lightning flashes and thunder peals; volcanos in all their violence of destruction; hurricanes with their track of devastation; the boundless ocean in a stage of tumult; the lofty waterfall of a mighty river. . .

Quite certainly Emily had not read *The Critique of Judgement,* but she had somehow, perhaps unconsciously, absorbed the widely discussed notions of the sublime which Kant, among others, had helped to shape and disseminate.

Earlier, in "A Philosophical Enquiry into the Origins of Our Ideas of the Sublime and Beautiful," Edmund Burke had linked beauty with the pleasurable response of attraction, and sublimity with a more complicated response involving pain and repulsion. In Part II of his widely read essay, he catalogued the conditions which evoked the sublime response in the beholder, and Emily Dickinson (again almost certainly without having read Burke or much literary theory at all) associated Awe with most of the qualities that he had mentioned and that had become criteria for the sublime: fear of danger and especially of death; privation (darkness, solitude, silence); obscurity and mystery; magnitude and infinity; suddenness.[56] While beauty had a self-subsisting and purposive harmony which was adapted to our judgment and imagination and which made the beautiful a source of restful satisfaction and pleasure, sublimity pained the judgment and imagination by exceeding their grasp and thus forced the mind to open out and strain to apprehend the over-powering object. Thereby the sublime raised "the energies of the soul above their accustomed height" to bring the infinite within its hold — almost but never quite. As Burke, Kant, and Schiller all concluded, the sublime gripped the mind more strongly than the beautiful precisely because it was an irresistible mixture of alternating (or perhaps simultaneous) delight and pain, exaltation and terror, attraction to the unknown and repulsion from the unknowable, as the individual grappled both to measure and to preserve himself against inscrutable forces. In Emerson's even more subjective and "mystical" paraphrase:

> . . . the emotion of the sublime . . . is an influx of the Divine mind into our mind. It is an ebb of the individual rivulet before the flowing surges of the sea of life. Every distinct apprehension of this central commandment agitates men with awe and delight.[57]

The romantic quest for *ultima Thule* explains a great deal about Emily Dickinson's fascination with things half seen and half hidden, and her wonder at "not precisely Knowing/ And not precisely Knowing not."[58] This was the sublime experience, and Awe united within itself the extremes of consciousness: "Transport's instability / And Doom's celerity"; or, as another poem phrased it, "the delicious throe / Of transport thrilled with Fear—"[59]

In 1884, at the end of her life, Emily Dickinson composed a quatrain * which drew together the themes of sexual, religious, and aesthetic fulfillment in the union of the bride and the knight, Circumference and Awe:

> Circumference thou Bride of Awe
> Possessing thou shalt be
> Possessed by every hallowed Knight **
> That dares to covet thee   (P 1620, III.1111)

The familiar terms establish the density of texture and reference which make so slight a poem carry so much force. There is an alternate last line, and when the poem is made to speak of the knight "that dares to covet thee" and "that bends a knee to thee," it stands even more emphatically as the final testament

---

* She sent the poem to Daniel Chester French, whom she had known briefly as a boy in Amherst, on the occasion of the unveiling of his statue of John Harvard in front of University Hall in Cambridge. It is one of the very few poems of Emily's written for an occasion.

** Cf. Thoreau's reference to the artist as a "captive knight": *A Week on the Concord and Merrimack Rivers*, p. 134.

to the multiple complexities which characterized (for Emily Dickinson at least) the life of consciousness: the ambivalence of the active and passive self in the pain and pleasure of experience. Here is the sublime culmination: within the awesome Circumference she is both bride and knight, each possessing and being possessed.

THE FLOWER, THE BEE,
AND THE SPIDER: THE
AESTHETICS OF CONSCIOUSNESS

I reckon — when I count at all —
First — Poets — Then the Sun —
Then Summer — Then the Heaven of God —
And then — the List is done —

But, looking back — the First so seems
To Comprehend the Whole —
The Others look a needless Show —
So I write — Poets — All —   (P 569, II.434)

WHEN Emily Dickinson bothered to count at all, she saw that the poet's Circumference comprehended the totality of experience. The statement is deceptive in one respect at least: the need to reassure herself of the incontrovertible rightness of her life's dedication impelled her to take count over and over again.

What was the poet's role? What was the function of poetry? To begin with, poetry permitted escape from pain, for pain found both relief and release in the distance and design imposed by artistic re-creation. In 1862 she wrote to Higginson: "I had

a terror — since September — I could tell to none — and so I sing,
as the Boy does by the Burying Ground — because I am afraid";
like her much admired Browning after his wife's death, she often
"sang off charnel steps." [1] Furthermore, by weaving pain into
pattern, the "Martyr Poet" rescued not just himself but fellow-
sufferers through time:

> The Martyr Poets — did not tell —
> But wrought their Pang in syllable —
> That when their mortal name be numb —
> Their mortal fate — encourage Some —
>
> .   .   .   .
>
> Some seek in Art — the Art of Peace —
> (P 544, II.417–18)

Poetry was a vehicle of pleasure as well as of pain, however,
and most of her theorizing (if that word can be applied to so
unsystematized a set of reactions) speculated about the interrela-
tionship of the poet, the experience, and the medium of artistic
expression. Was the artist essentially a passive seer, an assertive
genius, or a skilled craftsman? She might blithely say (and in the
thrall of the moment believe) that such questions were academic:

> The pedigree of Honey
> Does not concern the Bee,
> Nor lineage of Ecstasy
> Delay the Butterfly
> On spangled journeys to the peak
> Of some perceiveless thing —
> The right of way to Tripoli
> A more essential thing.   (P 1627, III.1116)

But here again she was pretending to shrug off a matter of basic
concern to her. After all, where was Tripoli and what was the
right of way? The origin and transmission and articulation of
inspiration were questions frequently propounded and never
finally answered. Poems themselves "exhibit here, as doth a

Burr," but the prickly question was: "Germ's Germ be where?" [2] Where and how is a poem conceived? Although Emily Dickinson gave various answers, they polarize around notions of the poet's function which correspond to the opposing tendencies that governed the course of her personal, religious, and emotional life.

The first notion of the poet is the common Romantic conception of the visionary, to which Emerson gave full endorsement in his essay on "The Poet":

This insight, which expresses itself by what is called Imagination, is a very high sort of seeing, which does not come by study, but by the intellect being where and what it sees; by sharing the path or circuit of things through forms, and so making them translucid to others . . . It is a secret which every intellectual man quickly learns, that beyond the energy of his possessed and conscious intellect he is capable of a new energy (as of an intellect doubled on itself), by abandonment to the nature of things; that beside his privacy of power as an individual man, there is a great public power on which he can draw, by unlocking, at all risks, his human doors, and suffering the ethereal tides to roll and circulate through him; then he is caught up in the life of the Universe . . .

The passive poet resigned himself "to the divine *aura* which breathes through forms." As in Wordsworth's poems and in Coleridge's more Wordsworthian poems, "the one Life within us and abroad" flowed together in a closed circuit; the distinction between subject and object was obliterated; the poet's "inward and outward senses [were] truly adjusted to each other"; his intellect moved out and doubled on itself. As Thoreau said, "Nature is mythical and mystical always . . ." Nature's "mysticism" is the "subtle magnetism . . . , which if we unconsciously yield to it, will direct us aright"; and myths are the scriptures which record symbolically the breath of "the God" in the poet, when "a superhuman intelligence" uses "the unconscious thoughts and dreams of man as its hieroglyphics." [3] In much the same way, Emily Dickinson saw that beauty was a quality

of Nature ("Beauty is nature's fact") and a part of man's inherent capacity ("Estranged from Beauty — none can be"), and
that in both its manifestations beauty was ultimately associated
with Being Itself ("Beauty — be not caused — It is — ").[4] She
could distinguish between the Dionysian seer (or listener) and
the Apollonian poet (or speaker):

> I would not talk, like Cornets —
> I'd rather be the One
> Raised softly to the Ceilings —
> And out, and easy on —
> Through Villages of Ether —
> .   .   .   .
>
> Nor would I be a Poet —
> It's finer — own the Ear —
> Enamored — impotent — content —
>
> (P 505, II.387–88)

The seer saw by the light of the divine lightning-flash,[5] the "One
— imperial — Thunderbolt — / That scalps your naked Soul."
Emily's gauge was immediate: "If I feel physically as if the top
of my head were taken off, I know *that* is poetry"[6]; and she repeated the idea in another poem:

> To pile like Thunder to it's close
> Then crumble grand away
> While Everything created hid
> This — would be Poetry —   (P 1247, III.866)

The trouble was, as always, that it did crumble away, and
the poet was left to try to communicate the fleeting experience
by its fading light. Shelley had trumpeted the visionary role of
the poet ("Poetry is indeed divine . . . at once the center and
circumference of knowledge"), and in "A Defence of Poetry"
he addressed himself to the problem of poetic articulation after
the inner blaze of inspiration:

A man cannot say, "I will compose poetry." The greatest poet even cannot say it; for the mind in creation is as a fading coal, which some invisible influence, like an unconstant wind, awakens to transitory brightness; this power arises from within, like the colour of a flower which fades and changes as it is developed . . . Could this influence be durable in its original purity and force, it is impossible to predict the greatness of the results; but when composition begins, inspiration is already on the decline, and the most glorious poetry that has ever been communicated to the world is probably a feeble shadow of the original conceptions of the poet.

With Yankee prudence Emily set out to transform the inescapable fact of the fading light into an advantage:

> By a departing light
> We see acuter, quite,
> Than by a wick that stays.
> There's something in the flight
> That clarifies the sight
> And decks the rays   (P 1714, III.1157)

So the "Habit — of a Laureate" was to find the flavor of experience (which was "metre," "melody," and "Poesy") the "spiciest at fading." Nevertheless, despite the intensity which the "departing light" affords, she had to admit that when the light fades, "True Poems flee": "To see the Summer Sky/ Is Poetry, though never in a Book it lie — " [7]

"True Poems flee," and only memory and language can hold them at all. But speech seems inadequate to report the "Reportless Subjects" and "Reportless Measures." Even so meticulous a craftsman as Marianne Moore has written: "Ecstasy affords/ the occasion and expediency determines the form"; and Emily Dickinson would have agreed: "It is the Ultimate of Talk —/ The Impotence to Tell." [8] When her "will endeavors for it's word/ And fails," then "Silence'[s] oblation to the Ear supersedes sound." As Thoreau remarked, in the poet's recollections in tranquillity "speech is fractional, silence is integral." Hawthorne had drawn the moral for "The Artist of the Beautiful": "When the artist rose high enough to achieve the beautiful, the symbol by which he made it perceptible to mortal senses became of little value in his eyes while his spirit possessed itself in the enjoyment of the reality."

How far was Emily Dickinson in her ecstasy of silence from the black Melvillean moods when "Silence is all we dread" and "There's Ransom in a Voice." [9] This Silence was fullness and not void. As Emerson had suggested, if one dared to open his human doors to the ethereal tides, one was seized by the god. This conception, shared by many of the English Romantics and the American Transcendentalists, places them in that tradition, which, coming down from the ancient oracles and Plato's *Ion*, viewed the poet as the unselfconscious interpreter of spiritual forces for the rest of society. So pervasive is the Romantic conception of the poet-medium that a latter-day transcendentalist like Henry Miller can reiterate the Emersonian position with unfaltering conviction (and note how extremely close this is to Emerson's statements):

Someone takes over and you just copy out what is being said . . . A writer shouldn't think much . . . I'm not very good at thinking. I work from some deep down place; and when I write, well, I don't know just exactly what's going to happen . . . Who writes the great books? It isn't we who sign our names. What is an artist? He's a man who has antennae, who knows how to hook up to the currents which are in the atmosphere, in the cosmos . . . Who is original? Everything that we are doing, everything that we think, exists already, and we are only intermediaries . . . [A writer should] recognize himself as a man who was possessed of a certain faculty which he was destined to use for the service of others. He has nothing to be proud of, his name means nothing, his ego is nil, he's only an instrument in a long procession.[10]

So the artist was divinely mad or divinely drunk. Emerson's poet was "inebriated by nectar . . . which is the ravishment of the intellect," and the poems "Bacchus" and "Merlin" describe his drunkenness; Thoreau spoke of the divine frenzy and the "bardic rage." In Amherst, too, there was a "little Tippler" who gave her account of the seraphic emancipation of "the New Liquor"[11]:

> I taste a liquor never brewed —
> From Tankards scooped in Pearl —
> Not all the Frankfort Berries
> Yield such an Alcohol!
>
> Inebriate of Air — am I —
> And Debauchee of Dew —
> Reeling — thro endless summer days —
> From inns of Molten Blue — (P 214, I.149)

It was a reeling triumph to be a secret drinker while in the name of orthodox religion her father labored tirelessly for the Temperance League. He could close the bars of Amherst, but not the "inns of Molten Blue" where she drank with saints and was served by angels.

Although the first premise was that the ecstatic eye of genius "beholds the design," Emerson (as did Shelley) quickly moved to the second: that the design existed "in an artist's mind, without flaw, mistake, or friction" before its execution into a work of art. Even this slight shift in emphasis made a great difference. After effusively hailing the poet-seer, the artist and the critic began to transfer the focus of attention from the divine efflux to the artist's heightened vision that determined the character of what he saw. In Thoreau's words:

Nature does not cast pearls before swine. There is just as much beauty visible to us in the landscape as we are prepared to appreciate, — not a grain more. The actual objects which one man will see from a particular hilltop are just as different from those another will see as the beholders are different. The Scarlet Oak must, in a sense, be in your eye when you go forth. We cannot see anything until we are possessed with the idea of it, take it into our heads, — and then we can hardly see anything else.[12]

In other words, the beholder's ideals and the beholder's vision predetermine his world. Pushed far enough, this line of thought led inescapably to Emerson's hypothesis that the "Universe was the externalization of the Soul" as the genius' shaping mind imprinted the plastic surface of Nature: "The genius is a genius by the first look he casts on any object. Is his eye creative?"; "Genius is the activity which repairs the decays of things . . ."

Emily Dickinson skirted the philosophical implications of the hypothesis, but, like the ego-oriented poet and unlike the mystic, she also quickly shifted her emphasis from the super-human force which possessed her to her power to possess Nature. The transition of perspective is accomplished, for example, in the following poem:

> Perception of an object costs
> Precise the Object's loss —
> Perception in itself a Gain
> Replying to it's Price —
> The Object Absolute — is nought —
> Perception sets it fair
> And then upbraids a Perfectness
> That situates so far — *   (P 1071, II.757)

* Alternate line: that 'tis so Heavenly far —

She is concerned not with the "Perfectness" of the ultimate reality "that 'tis so Heavenly far," nor with the object, which is "nought" in itself, but with the poet's perception, which more than compensates for the sacrifice of the negligible phenomenal existence. In Wallace Stevens' statement of much the same idea, the artist answers the challenge that "You do not play things as they are" upon the blue guitar with the unequivocal reply that "Things as they are/ Are changed upon the blue guitar." Similarly, Emily exulted that she, and not Nature nor the experience itself, determined meaning:

> To hear an Oriole sing
> May be a common thing —
> Or only a divine.
>
> . . . .
>
> So whether it be Rune,
> Or whether it be none
> Is of within.
>
> The "Tune is in the Tree —"
> The Skeptic — showeth me —
> "No Sir! In Thee!"   (P 526, II.404)

The angelic Debauchee found that "of juleps, part are in the Jug/ And more are in the joy." At times so subjective was her perception and response that she seemed able to dispense with the encumbrance of Nature: "I saw the sunrise on the Alps since I saw you. Travel why to Nature, when she dwells with us? Those who lift their hats shall see her, as devout do God." [13]

At such moments she talked not about being scalped by God's imperial thunderbolt but about "the Art to stun myself/ With Bolts of Melody!" When she felt that "The Outer — from the Inner/ Derives it's Magnitude," she spoke metaphorically not of ravishment by the lightning but of the incendiary energies of "my volcano" within:

> How red the Fire rocks below
> How insecure the sod
> Did I disclose
> Would populate with awe my solitude
>   (P 1677, III.1141)

If she unleashed the explosive force, "hissing Corals part — and shut —/ And Cities — ooze away." Consequently she avoided the public demonstration of an eruption and kept the lava seething in the deeps:

The reticent volcano keeps
His never slumbering plan;
Confided are his projects pink
To no precarious man.

.   .   .   .

Admonished by her * buckled lips
Let every babbler be
The only secret people keep
Is Immortality.   (P 1748, III.1174)

By choice and by titanic control she reserved herself to "con-template/ Vesuvius at Home." [14]

There are other metaphors to express the quandary of the "Inner" and the "Outer" force in images more suggestive of a timid feminine sensibility than the lightning and the volcano, though these patterns too have ambivalent sexual overtones. The very earliest poems [15] enunciate the terms simply and directly. In one poem she seeks her Master's bed; in another, she cringes at his feet; in still another she is "ravished" by the April day. On the other hand, there are poems in which she masters Nature in what is clearly in her own mind a rape: "I robbed the Woods—/ The trusting Woods"; she plucked the blossom and "bore her struggling, blushing,/ Her simple haunts beyond!" The early poems also introduce the problem through the symbol-ism of the flower and the bee: images which in their variation throughout her writing dramatize the poet's duality.

The flower, most often the rose or the daisy, becomes the em-blem of her yearning to be delivered up to the domination of a Master and, in the aesthetic order, corresponds to a conception of herself as the passive visionary gripped by the god. Hence her pleas: "Pray gather me—/ Anemone—/ Thy flower forever-more!"; "Then take my flowers — pray!" [16] For

---

* Note the significant shift from masculine to feminine pronoun as she identified herself more closely with the volcano.

137

> till the Bee
> Blossoms stand negative,
> Touched to Conditions
> By a Hum.   (P 1042, II.737–38)

The humming touch, however, works immediate magic, transfiguring the botanical specimen to a radiant rose:

> A sepal, petal, and a thorn
> Upon a common summer's morn —
> A flask of Dew — A Bee or two —
> A Breeze — a caper in the trees —
> And I'm a Rose!   (P 19, I.21)

When Emily identified herself with the blossom, it seemed to her that "to be a Flower, is profound/ Responsibility," [17] and at such times her only complaint was a familiar one — that the bee was a deceitful Master, a casual lover who loved her only to leave her godless again:

> His Suit a chance
> His Troth a Term
> Protracted as the Breeze
> Continual Ban propoundeth He
> Continual Divorce.   (P 896, II.660)

On other occasions Emily Dickinson liked to fancy herself the bee quaffing Nature's nectar, like Emerson's "Humble-Bee" (which was one of her favorite poems). Soon the bee was playing a more authoritative role, and the transition follows that in this passage from Thoreau: "How to extract its honey from the flower of the world — that is *my* every-day business. I am as busy as a bee about it. Do I not impregnate and intermix the flowers, produce rarer and finer varieties, by transferring my eyes from one to another? It is with flowers I would deal." [18] As Thoreau shifted from tasting the flower of the world to impregnating the flowers of the world, so Emily could not rest in the rose's ability "to subdue the Bumblebee" nor in the bee's mere savoring of the rose for its sweetness. It was (in Hopkins' phrase) "the achieve of, the mastery of the thing" that she finally had to have for herself: "Oh, for a Bee's experience/ Of Clovers" whose humming touch animated the "negative" flowers.[19] In aesthetic terms, the bee's experience corresponded to the prerogative of the genius' power over Nature, his ability to vanquish and to pollinate inert phenomena:

> Like Trains of Cars on Tracks of Plush
> I hear the level Bee —
> A Jar across the Flowers goes
> Their Velvet Masonry
>
> Withstands until the sweet Assault
> Their Chivalry consumes —
> While He, victorious tilts away
> To vanquish other Blooms.   (P 1224, III.852)

Emily Dickinson could think of herself as the flower or the bee, as the poet possessed or the poet possessing. Since she was no stickler for logic or rigid theory, the point is not that these concepts of the poet existed for her as distinct abstract categories but, on the contrary, that in living poetically she knew both experiences and appropriated both roles:

> Because the Bee may blameless hum
> For Thee a Bee do I become
> List even unto Me.
>
> Because the Flowers unafraid
> May lift a look on thine, a Maid
> Alway a Flower would be.   (P 869, II.647)

After a poem which she entitled "The Bumble Bee's Religion" (P 1522 III.1049) and in which she sympathized with the bee, she assumed the flower's role and appended two inscriptions. The first precept (purportedly from Jonathan Edwards) — "All

Liars shall have their part" — condemns the bee's deceitful rape, but the second — "And let him that is athirst come" — re-issues the flower's invitation.

If the conception of the poet is allowed to evolve even further in the direction of the bee, he becomes an increasingly self-empowered agent. In the twentieth century Wallace Stevens would posit the poet's mind as the only source of order over a chaotic nature:

> What is divinity if it can come
> Only in silent shadows and in dreams?
>
> . . . .
>
> Divinity must live within herself:
>
> . . . .
>
> All pleasures and all pains, remembering
> The bough of summer and the winter branch.
> These are the measures destined for her soul.*

Emily Dickinson was not always so subjective, but for her too, when the "Dream recedes — unrealized — " it is the poet's task to realize it.[20] He must distill

> amazing sense
> From ordinary Meanings —
> And Attar so immense
>
> From the familiar species
> That perished by the Door —
>
> (P 448, I.346)

And paradoxically he must destroy the common rose in order to press from it the precious attar:

> Essential Oils — are wrung —
> The Attar from the Rose
> Be not expressed by Suns — alone —
> It is the gift of Screws —   (P 675, II.522)

* From "Sunday Morning," *Collected Poems* (New York: Alfred A. Knopf, 1955), p. 67.

In this attempt to describe the poetic process in familiar images, the rose symbolizes natural phenomena; the sun, the transcendent fertilizing power; and the attar, the artistic distillation. From this point of view art is not a matter of simple reproduction of natural objects nor even of divine inspiration but rather a distinctly human process of destruction and creation in which the artist makes from the materials of nature something new and superior. The focus of discussion is shifting now from a consideration of the creative eye of genius to that of the creative hand of the craftsman. It is only by the requisite training and skill that the artist can practice his trade, and so it is the artist as artisan who finally wrings the attar from the rose.

If Nature seemed to the artist "a Haunted House," art was "a House that tries to be haunted"; that is, if the artist's eye perceived Nature as animated by divine forces, his task was to invest his work with spirits. Often, however, experience seemed to refute the transcendental doctrine:

> Nature assigns the Sun —
> That — is Astronomy —
> Nature cannot enact a Friend —
> That — is Astrology.   (P 1336, III.923)

In this case, if Nature was matter empty of spirit, if divinity withdrew so that none "passed her haunted house,/ Nor simplified her ghost,"[21] the artist had an even more demanding role. He had to raise imaginative spirits — perhaps invent them — for the haunted house of Art; he had to make magic by sleight-of-hand; in Marianne Moore's phrase, he had to present "imaginary gardens" for his "real toads."

The proximity to and separation from Nature's haunted house are Emily's unsophisticated terms for the distinction which Schiller had made between kinds of poets in his influential essay "On Simple and Sentimental Poetry." The Dickinson

library contained two sets of Schiller's *Works*, but whether or
not Emily actually read his critical views, she had arrived somehow, probably instinctively, at the point and substance of his
conclusions. According to Schiller, the simple poet — say, Homer
or Shakespeare — is in harmony with Nature and expresses its
ideals and truths unconsciously, with spontaneous response in
natural forms. In his peculiar use of the word "sentimental," the
sentimental poet — Goethe, for example, or Schiller himself —
finds that he is in opposition to nature or at any rate alienated
from it, so that only out of the individual consciousness, thrown
back on itself and struggling for comprehension, would emerge
the inspiration, the vision, and the complex forms which would
remake nature and elevate it into art. Although the civilized art
of modern cultures was becoming increasingly sentimental,
something of the difference between the receptive poet of Nature
and the self-conscious genius (never, of course, an exclusive
disjunction) can be suggested by the juxtaposition of Wordsworth
and Byron, or, in American poetry, by that of Emerson and Melville or Poe.

But whether transcendentalist or not, whether astrologist or
astronomer, simple poet or sentimental, seer or genius, it was the
artist's performance that revealed him as a maker-creator "able
as a God": "Himself — to Him — a Fortune — / Exterior — to
Time." Emily Dickinson's boast was that "Myself was formed
— a Carpenter," who wrought from her materials not buildings
but temples; her exultation was that the tireless practice of her
trade yielded to her the Kingdom, the Power, and the Glory.[22]

A poet could not be only a seer, but was, by compulsion and
by profession, a sayer as well — or, in Emerson's phrase, a "Namer
or Language-maker." As the oracular seer, Emerson did say that
"it was not metres, but a metre-making argument that makes a
poem" and that "the thought and the form are equal in the order
of time, but in the order of genesis the thought is prior to the

form." Not even Emerson, however, was unconcerned with form or structure. What he wanted was form that proceeded from, and was determined by, the materials themselves. Content took precedence over form — but only in the order of genesis. The real problem for the artist was to communicate the unique experience — sense impressions, flashes of perception, emotional responses — in an utterly different and artificial medium — for the poet, through related and patterned words. Such communication, *"alter idem,* in a manner totally new,"[23] though distinct from the generating experience, was nonetheless an organic outgrowth of the experience. Expert control of the medium incarnated the experience without forfeiting its essential character or aura. The artistic process, one might even say, was a kind of Transubstantiation in which the intangible substance was made present and communal in the palpable guise of words and sentences. Emerson made the analogy between the poem and the Sacrament in "Bacchus," and Emily Dickinson invoked it to bless her vocation:

> A Word made Flesh is seldom
> And tremblingly partook
> Nor then perhaps reported
> But have I not mistook
> Each one of us has tasted
> With ecstasies of stealth
> The very food debated
> To our specific strength —
>
> A Word that breathes distinctly
> Has not the power to die
> Cohesive as the Spirit
> It may expire if He —
> "Made Flesh and dwelt among us
> Could condescension be
> Like this consent of Language
> This loved Philology   (P 1651, III.1129)

143

The first stanza associates Christ's Incarnation with individual epiphanies; the second proceeds to the aesthetic process which incarnates the individual epiphany in words and concludes that in a hierarchical scale the precipitation into language (this beloved philology) is the final analogue to the divine condescension.

Since organic expression works by transmutation, if not by Transubstantiation, it must operate by "wonderful indirections," in which words are made to correspond to the movements of eye, head, and heart. "Tell all the Truth," Emily instructed herself, "but tell it slant —/ Success in Circuit lies." When she said that "every suggestion is Dimension," she was really referring to what she called on another occasion "the circumference of Expression," and was thereby assigning to form and style all the connotations of the word "circumference": self-contained fullness and totality; precision of outline and bounds; circuitous definition of center and dimension. In her mind the Bible, unlike poetry, spoke "with the Centre, not with the Circumference" of expression,[24] because the Bible made emphatic, direct statements about God (the omnipresent Center) in God's own words, whereas poetry could only speak roundabout in her own words. So clearly did she realize that the particular style and form which a poet used was a projection of himself and his experience that she rejected — politely and gratefully but adamantly — every piece of practical literary advice that "Preceptor" Higginson offered.

What, then, was the basic element in the peculiar and distinctive style which Emily Dickinson made? Emerson had said that organic form depended on making every nuance of relation into a new word; the poet named things "sometimes after their appearance, sometimes after their essence," and gave "to every one its own name and not another's, thereby rejoicing the intellect, which delights in detachment or boundary." We might often want more conciseness and particularity in Emerson's style, but Emily's friend Dr. Holland expressed a popular contemporary view when he observed of Emerson's writing: "There is no more spare language on his ideas, than there is flesh on his bones corporeal. A word less on the one, or an atom less on the other, and there would be a fatal catastrophe." In his journal Thoreau had formulated this same first commandment for the stylist: "By your few words show how insufficient would be many words . . . In breadth we may be patterns of conciseness, but in depth we may well be prolix." [25] Emily Dickinson refined this tendency toward exactness and condensation even further. If Emerson and Thoreau wrote at their best in well-wrought and precisely tooled sentences, then Emily Dickinson compressed language into finely honed and deliberately placed words. Her mind did not move in abstract or even sequential logic, and so her language — whether in verse or prose — does not depend on its sweep or smoothness or exuberance or delicately woven texture or even on its syntactical coherence. Indeed, the very confusion of the syntax — a fairly common occurrence, actually — forces the reader to concentrate on the basic verbal units and derive the strength and meaning largely from the circumference of words.

Therefore, while as the poet-seer she could bewail the inadequacy of words for the vision, as poet-craftsman she reveled time and again in the breadth and depth enclosed in one mighty word:

> Could mortal lip divine
> The undeveloped Freight
> Of a delivered syllable
> 'Twould crumble with the weight.
>
> (P 1409, III.978)

Moreover, her concern was not just with the density or weight of the words but with the "life and palpitation" which Thoreau called for:

A word is dead
When it is said,
Some say.
I say it just
Begins to live
That day.   (P 1212, III.845)

The vigorous word lived primarily in itself — in its sensual con-
creteness or its conceptual precision or its connotative resonance
or its metaphorical implications — but secondarily it lived in its
effect on the verse pattern — that is, in its contribution to rhyme,
rhythm, alliteration, and so on. "How lovely," Emily exclaimed
to Mrs. Holland, "are the wiles of Words!" [26]

Despite her indebtedness to Emerson, Emily Dickinson's
verse is not Emersonian. Like Schiller's sentimental poet and
unlike Emerson's artist in "The Snow-Storm," she knew that
art had more to do than merely mimic the "frolic architecture"
of Nature. When it came to specific matters of approach and
technique, when it came to writing a poem and practicing her
craft, she did not belong to the prophetic or Dionysian strain
of American poetry which derived palely from Emerson and
descended lustily through Whitman to Carl Sandburg and Jeffers, and more recently to Jack Kerouac and Brother Antoninus.
If for the moment's convenience American poetry may be divided broadly into opposing tendencies, the deliberate and for-
malistic quality of Dickinson's verse associates her rather with
the diverse yet Apollonian tradition which proceeds from Edward Taylor through her to Eliot, Stevens, Frost, and Marianne
Moore, and thence to Robert Lowell and Elizabeth Bishop. The
dynamic energies of Whitman's language open out to shatter
the form and "stand witness to a world beyond the world of his
making." [27] No matter what Emily Dickinson might say about
the poet's vatic function, the dynamic energies of her language
close tightly to assert the presence of an aesthetic object of the
poet's making.

A good indication of her formalism is her insatiable and un-abating interest in the wiles of words (again one thinks of Mar-ianne Moore *). Emily told Higginson that for some years her lexicon had been her only companion, and throughout her life she pored over the dictionary as zealously as she read her Bible. From the native strength of words and from her experiments in expanding their scope she fashioned a unique language (Hig-ginson thought it "spasmodic" and "uncontrolled." [28]) She chose words with stinging freshness; she flavored speech with earthy New England colloquialisms; she often dropped the "s" of the third-person singular of the present tense to suggest the enduring quality of the action; she emphasized nouns by the striking addi-tion or omission of the preceding article; she sometimes used singular nouns where plurals were expected and vice versa; she made parts of speech perform unorthodox functions, used words in startling contexts, coined words when none seemed available or apt.[29] Like Ezra Pound, William Carlos Williams, Marianne Moore, and E. E. Cummings, Emily Dickinson sought to speak the uniqueness of her experience in a personal tongue by recon-stituting and revitalizing — at the risk of eccentricity — the basic verbal unit.

For the framework in which to set her words, Emily Dickin-son came naturally to depend on the standard hymn stanzas. She was familiar with them from church and was otherwise quite unsophisticated in the technicalities of metrics. The quatrains of short lines (mostly three and four beats) imposed the necessity

* See Miss Moore's "To a Snail":
> If 'compression is the first grace of style,'
> you have it. Contractility is a virtue
> as modesty is a virtue.

> . . . .

> in the absence of feet, 'a method of conclusions';
> 'a knowledge of principles',
> in the curious phenomenon of your occipital horn.

(Reprinted with permission of The Macmillan Co. from *Collected Poems* by Marianne Moore, New York, 1951, p. 91. Copyright 1935 by Marianne Moore; renewed 1963 by Marianne Moore and T. S. Eliot.)

for conciseness and control, and the association with the meetinghouse suggested (whether she realized it or not) the religious
basis of her poetic calling. Without relaxing the rigid formality
of the quatrains she gave them variety and adaptability through
the flexibility of the rhythms (marked by those dots and dashes
that serve as breathing points) and through the atonality of slant
rimes and the internal harmonics of the vowels and consonants.
She had worked out a stanza which was prescribed without
monotony and which could be skillfully worked within strict
limits.

Take for example this carefully constructed quatrain:

> The Clock strikes one that just struck two —
> Some schism in the Sum —
> A Vagabond from Genesis
> Has wrecked the Pendulum —   (P 1569, III. 1081)

All the words are monosyllables except for three trisyllabic words
(Vagabond, Genesis, Pendulum), and these are reiterated in
the trisyllabic rime "in the Sum" and in the three words beginning with "s" in the second line. The tone of the bell "strikes
one" in the monosyllables and especially in the words "Clock,"
"strikes," "struck," and "wrecked." The "two" mentioned at the
end of the first line is repeated in the "Some" and "Sum" of the
second, which are in turn split by "schism." In the poem which
begins "When Bells stop ringing — Church — begins —" (P 633
II.486, quoted in full in the previous chapter) the slow, solemn
pace suggests the motionlessness which is the subject of the
poem. Another quatrain is built on the tonal possibilities of the
letter "o," on which every change is rung:

> The blonde Assassin passes on —
> The Sun proceeds unmoved
> To measure off another Day
> For an Approving God.   (P 1624, III.1114)

148

A more complex sound pattern becomes a chamber of echoes, in which "b," "l," and "e" tumble in rapid succession and the short "i"'s of the first line are picked up in the last:

> Admonished by her buckled lips
> Let every babbler be
> The only secret people keep
> Is Immortality. (P 1748, III.1174)

This sort of analysis might best be left to the explorations of the individual reader of the poetry, especially since the point is by now plain. Like a good American craftsman, Emily Dickinson whittled her materials, within the limits of a rather strict form, into something of beauty and use. Moreover, the qualities of her style attest to the qualities of her consciousness; at its best the writing is terse, compact, concrete — and yet oblique, cryptic, surrendering its secret only in lightning-flashes of word and metaphor.

The artist had to expend time on craft because it supplied what all experience, even ecstasy, lacked — namely, permanence. The dexterous craftsman who carved a well-fitted and self-contained creation elevated himself above mutability, and like Poe's artist who was god of his own creation, decreed his own immortality:

> When Orient have been outgrown —
> And Occident — become Unknown —
> His Name — remain — (P 307, I.228)

This is an old theme, but for those who, like Keats, Dickinson, and Thoreau, sought "no higher heaven than . . . a *purely* sensuous life" of consciousness, it had poignant and compelling urgency. "Every author," said Thoreau in his journal, "writes in the faith that his book is to be the final resting place of the sojourning soul, and sets up his fixtures therein as for a more than oriental permanence . . ."[30]

The supreme act of transcendence which the structure of *Walden* represents is made explicit at the "Conclusion" in the parable of the artist of Kouroo. By taking the time and care to carve a perfect staff with "singleness of purpose and resolution" and with "elevated piety," he had escaped the tyranny of time in a temporal apotheosis:

> When the finishing stroke was put to his work, it suddenly expanded before the eyes of the astonished artist into the fairest of all the creations of Brahma. He had made a new system in making the staff, a world of full and fair proportions . . . . The material was pure, and his art was pure; how could the result be other than wonderful?

Wallace Stevens would say of his singing woman in "The Idea of Order at Key West":

> . . . she was the maker of the song she sang.
> The ever-hooded, tragic-gestured sea
> Was merely a place by which she walked to sing.
>
> . . . .
>
> She was the single artificer of the world
> In which she sang.*

When Emily Dickinson spoke of the attar made from the decaying rose which

> in Lady's Drawer
> Make Summer — When the Lady lie
> In Ceaseless Rosemary —   (P 675, II.522)

she was thinking of the sheafs of poems in her drawer waiting to be found when her body was laid "in Ceaseless Rosemary." Since her immortality depended on it, she hoped that she, like Thoreau and his artist of Kouroo, had made "a new system," "a world of full and fair proportions"; for then her poems would

* From "The Idea of Order at Key West," in *Collected Poems* (New York: Alfred A. Knopf, 1955), p. 129.

Inhere as do the Suns —
Each Age a Lens
Disseminating their
Circumference —   (P 883, II.654)

The spider is Emily Dickinson's emblem for the craftsman spinning from within himself his sharply defined world. The spider image occurs throughout American writing with revealing differences in image and association. There is the simple emblem of Taylor's "Upon a Spider Catching a Fly," and Jonathan Edwards' spider-sinner in the hands of an angry God. Whitman sees the spider as the individual threading himself to the cosmos; Frost suggests the spider's ambiguous involvement in an amoral "Design," and Robert Lowell makes use of Edwards' spider as the complex but unifying metaphor for man's tragic condition. Emily Dickinson's spider is none of these. He is "an Artist," whose "unperceived Hands" mysteriously and skillfully weave tapestries from the private resource of his hidden "Yarn of Pearl" [31] — tapestries whose beauty and design originated in himself. Swift had scorned the spider's insubstantial web woven from his own filth and excrement and extolled the bee's sweetness and light, but Emily gladly sympathized with the spider-artist: "Neglected Son of Genius / I take thee by the Hand — "

It could seem to her that in a dark world the lonely spider-artist worked in bright circumference:

A Spider sewed at Night
Without a Light
Upon an Arc of White.

If Ruff it was of Dame
Or Shroud of Gnome
Himself himself inform.

Of Immortality
His Strategy
Was Physiognomy.   (P 1138, II.800)

The second stanza says that only the poet knows what he is doing; it also says that in his writing he is "informing" himself in the sense of "giving form to" a projected image of himself. There are two poets ("Himself himself inform"): the creator catches his experience in a web of words. His strategy for immortality, she writes, is "Physiognomy": the design spun of and from himself to outwit night and death. Thus Emily Dickinson marked a turning point in the American poet's conception of his function. For all her experience of the blaze of noon and the lightning-flash, for all her knowledge of the flower's ecstasy and the bee's power, she had to reject the kind of "mysticism" which in Emerson became mistiness and in Whitman amorphousness. She wrote neither as a visionary nor as a genius but as a craftsman making order out of the fragments of mutability. The only question was how durable one's web was; and durability depended on how well one practiced one's "Trade." She could only trust with Thoreau and Keats * that if the materials and the art were pure, the result could not be other than wonderful.

* Keats, too, invoked the flower, the bee, and the spider with associations strikingly like Emily's; see Walter Jackson Bate, *John Keats* (Cambridge, Massachusetts, 1963), pp. 250–252.

THE TIGHTENING CIRCLE

Throughout her life, on various levels of experience, through the wide range of her poetry, Emily Dickinson was raising the same fundamental question: Is there an objective correspondence between the beholder and the beheld? Do I know myself only in connection with, even in submission to, something beyond self? Or must I make my own meaning in a murky universe? Furthermore, when I behold Nature, is there an inherent correlation between the phenomenon and its significance, between the concrete thing and its universal relevance, between physics and metaphysics? Her answers were momentary acts of living, and in the existential acts of consciousness her hesitation between alternatives, her testing of both alternatives, mark her unique and crucial position in the history of the American mind and imagination.

When addressed specifically to the imagination, the question is whether Nature is type or trope. As Perry Miller has pointed out, "the habit of finding symbols of the abstract in the concrete was a part of the literary tradition from the days of the first masters, Thomas Hooker, John Cotton, and Thomas Shepard." Their "emblems" and "sermons in stone" took natural objects to be types of a transcendent truth. Types were not mere allegories or fictions or figures of speech; they comprised a special kind of symbol whose expression of the abstract was the reason and purpose of the object's existence, so that the primary importance of the type was to reflect the essential analogy with the anti-type (that is, the higher truth). By contrast, tropes were metaphors or similes; the connection between the object and its meaning depended not on an objective correspondence between the two but on the mental agility of the writer who made the association and used the figure to illuminate or illustrate his point. "In the type there must be evidence of the one eternal intention; in the trope there can be evidence only of the intention of one writer."[1] Puritans like Hooker and Cotton did not scorn tropes; however, while they found them effective in discourse, they maintained a strict distinction between tropes employed to clarify the truth of scriptural doctrine and the typological manifestation of Truth Itself in the contingent workings of creation. To see the distinction, one need only contrast the highly tropological rhetoric of Cotton Mather with (on the simplest level) the interpretation of types in the Puritan diaries or (more gloriously) Samuel Sewall's apostrophe to Plum Island, in which the fertile beauty of the American wilderness becomes the type of the prayer "Thy kingdom come."

Edwards' ardent approach to the natural world is premised upon its typological revelation:

Again it is apparent and allowed that there is a great and remarkable analogy in God's works. There is a wonderful resemblance in the effects which God produces, and consentaneity in His manner of working in one thing and another throughout all nature. It is very observable in the visible world . . . And if so, why should not we suppose that He makes the inferiour in imitation of the superiour, the material of the spiritual, on purpose to have a resemblance and shadow of them? We see that even in the material world, God makes one part of it strangely to agree with another, and why is it not reasonable to suppose He makes the whole as a shadow of the spiritual world?[2]

He went on to explain that "if the sowing of seed and its spring-ing were not designedly ordered to have an agreeableness to the resurrection, there could be no sort of argument in that which the Apostle alledges . . . See how the Apostle's argument is thus founded (Heb. 9.16,17) upon the validity of a testament." Nature, Scripture, philosophy, and theology were only different revelations of the self-existent Truth. Newton had taught him that he had to relate his physics to his theology; Locke had taught him that knowledge originated in sense impressions. One had to know the universe as matter, one had to know objects as con-crete things, before phenomena could be seized intuitively as "images, or shadows of divine things." So, too, verbal communi-cation relied either on the explication of types which embody the truth or on the construction of tropes to give flesh to an ab-straction and make it a living experience, or, as Edwards called it, "a naked idea." The particular image became, in one sense or the other, the medium for the universal truth.

From this point of view it is not far from Edwards' premises to Emerson's axioms:

1. Words are signs of natural facts.
2. Particular natural facts are symbols of particular spiritual facts.
3. Nature is the symbol of spirit.[3]

The difference arose when Emerson said that "the possibility of interpretation lies in the identity of the observer with the ob-served. Each material thing has its celestial side; has its trans-lation, through humanity, into the spiritual and necessary sphere . . ." He insisted on the typology, but translated "through hu-manity." It is true that in a famous sentence in *Nature* Emerson advocated fastening "words again to visible things" and thereby to their typological significance, but what he really meant is ex-pressed in the very next sentence when he said that, under the stimulus of thought or passion, discourse "clothes itself in images." By jettisoning not only theology but an epistemological, cosmological, and metaphysical frame, he made types depend on individual perception and on the individual imagination and so blurred the sharply marked distinction between type and trope. This subjectivity soon posed insoluble problems in establishing the absolute validity of the ideal order and even of the existence of the cosmos outside the mind. Emerson might circumvent the difficulties with the pragmatic admonition to act as though the world were real, whether it was or not. Nevertheless, the relations between the perceiver, the perceived, and the perception had been profoundly disturbed — cut loose, in fact, from any anchoring standard of judgment — so that it is not surprising to find Emerson speaking of Nature as type, and using natural images as tropes. All too rarely did he approach Nature to penetrate to the universal through the absorption of the immediate; instead, Emerson's inclination was to enliven his ideas with striking images.

For all Thoreau's exultation in the primitive and palpable sense of things, the journals (like the writings of Wordsworth and Emerson after their first outbursts of inspiration) came more and more to be a dogged but flagging struggle to invoke again "the visionary gleam . . . the glory and the dream." * *Walden* and Whitman's *Leaves of Grass* were the last successful efforts in the nineteenth century to sustain the balance between the concrete and the universal through an entire major work, for Emerson's "noble doubt" (or what Whitman called "the terrible doubt of appearances") had so undermined the foundations of an ob-

---

* See this entry as early as 1850: "I fear that the character of my knowledge is from year to year becoming more distinct and scientific; that, in exchange for views as wide as heaven's eye, I am being narrowed down to the field of the microscope" (*Journals*, II, 406). Or this from 1852: "Once I was part and parcel of Nature [Emerson's phrase from *Nature*]; now I am observant of her" (*Journals*, III, 378).

jective typology that even Thoreau and Whitman could hold the precarious equilibrium only in terms of the omnipresent "I." And here, while the impulse in both cases might allegedly be to identify the "I" with external objects, the lingering impression is that objects have been transformed into the counters of consciousness.

Although William Cullen Bryant might try to see the flight of the waterfowl as a pale type of Providence, Poe said that meaning was a matter of the artist's contrivance. Soon Hawthorne was claiming the prerogative to distort the natural world and color it with his imagination in order to suggest the complex and private reality, and if to Hawthorne "the truth of the human heart" was psychologically and morally complex, it was to Melville bafflingly ambiguous — "one pervading ambiguity the only possible explanation for all the ambiguous details." Consequently, by mid-century Melville had already come to the point of declaring:

Say what some poets will, Nature is not so much her own eversweet interpreter, as the mere supplier of that cunning alphabet, whereby selecting and combining as he pleases, each man reads his own peculiar lesson according to his own peculiar mind and mood.[4]

Not everyone found the human predicament as inscrutable as Melville did, but his vehemence sounded his alarm at the schism that was widening between experience and meaning, life and literature, nature and art. Later Henry James made his own assessment:

Life being all inclusion and confusion, and art being all discrimination and selection, the latter, in search of the hard latent *value* with which alone it is concerned, sniffs around the mass as instinctively and unerringly as a dog suspicious of some buried bone . . . the artist finds in *his* tiny nugget, washed free of awkward accretions and hammered into a sacred hardness, the very stuff for a clear affirmation, the happiest chance for the indestructible.[5]

And, James continued, since art is nourished by "its fairly living on the sincere and shifting experience of the individual practicioner," since it is peculiarly "*his* tiny nugget" to be hammered into art, "I live, live intensely, and am fed by life, and my value, whatever it may be, is in my own kind of expression of that." Through selection and reconstruction art "*makes* life, makes interest, makes importance . . . and I know of no substitute whatever for the force and beauty of its process." [6]

Soon, for many twentieth-century writers, as for Melville, even the hard nugget of truth became hopelessly lost in the confusion of experience. Frost, looking down a well into the heart of nature, wrote with wry skepticism of the pebble he thought he saw at the bottom:

> *Once*, when trying with chin against a well-curb,
> I discerned, as I thought, beyond the picture,
> Through the picture, a something white, uncertain,
> Something more of the depths — and then I lost it.
> Water came to rebuke the too clear water.
> One drop fell from a fern, and lo, a ripple
> Shook whatever it was lay there at bottom,
> Blurred it, blotted it out. What was that whiteness?
> Truth? A pebble of quartz? For once, then, something.*

For Robert Frost poetry was the form in which he could articulate the irony of ambiguity. In Wallace Stevens the disjunction between the real and the ideal, between experience and meaning, became the central concern of his poetry. There was no shape to the weltering world he saw; in "The Man with the Blue Guitar" only the inventive imagination seemed able to allow repose in the order of its own designs:

* Robert Frost, *Complete Poems* (New York: 1949), p. 276. Copyright 1916, 1921, 1923 by Holt, Rinehart and Winston, Inc. Copyright 1942, 1944, 1951 by Robert Frost. Reprinted by permission of Holt, Rinehart and Winston, Inc.

I cannot bring a world quite round,
Although I patch it as I can.

.   .   .   .

The earth, for us, is flat and bare.
There are no shadows. Poetry

Exceeding music must take the place
Of empty heavens and its hymns,

Ourselves in poetry must take their place,
Even in the chattering of your guitar.

.   .   .   .

For a moment final, in the way
The thinking of art seems final when
The thinking of god is smoky dew.*

"Modern reality," Stevens once noted, "is a reality of de-crea-
tion, in which our revelations are not the revelations of belief
but the precious portents of our own powers." Though the imagination must draw its images from objects, the poem often turns
not on things but on imaginative abstractions from things:
"Poetry is the subject of the poem," and "The Ultimate Poem Is
Abstract." [7]

Among poets, Wallace Stevens is not so abstract in his use of
words as Gertrude Stein or Edith Sitwell. He was a poet of the
imagination, and his imagination had to draw upon external
reality. And yet in his flamboyant inventiveness, in his technical
finesse, in his absorption in art, there was an element which suggested the final disintegration of the Romantic aesthetic: the
danger that the imagination (Coleridge would have insisted that
it was only the fancy) would become trapped in the turns of its
own tropes. Stevens worried about the danger more deeply than
his critics, and raised the question against himself in "The Man
on the Dump." The world-dump of this poem is utterly lacking

* From *Collected Poems* (New York: Alfred A. Knopf, 1955), pp. 165,
167, and 168.

in any "hard latent *value*" such as James strove to extract from the confusion. With unsparing eye Stevens depicted the poet sitting atop the dump, picking among the rubbish and deluding himself with his own illusions:

> Is it a philosopher's honeymoon, one finds
> On the dump? Is it to sit among the mattresses of the dead,
> Bottles, pots, shoes and grass and murmur *aptest eve*:
> Is it to hear the blatter of grackles and say
> *Invisible priest*; is it to eject, to pull
> The day to pieces and cry *stanza my stone*?*

If the imaginative *mundo* has no reference beyond itself, then is not art mere polished and decorative surfaces? Stoically refusing such illusory consolations, Stevens returned to objective reality again and again [8] with the determination to relate the world and his *mundo*. In "The Poems of Our Climate,"

> The imperfect is our paradise.
> Note that, in this bitterness, delight
> Since the imperfect is so hot in us,
> Lies in flawed words and stubborn sounds.**

It is a long way from the Puritans' "sermons in stones" to Stevens' "*stanza my stone*," and, in between, Emily Dickinson occupies a central place. She felt the impulse to find outside herself something which answered her and which she could answer, yet she cringed at the "awful daring of a moment's surrender/ Which an age of prudence can never retract . . . ," even though she feared that by this surrender "and this only, we have existed." Emerson had flatly assured a response if one dared to unlock "at all risks, his human doors," but how could she be sure? Intellectually she lacked the conviction that would sustain the risk; personally, the boldness that would take the risk; emotionally, the stability that would absorb the risk. So,

* *Collected Poems* (New York: Alfred A. Knopf, 1955), p. 203.
** *Ibid.*, p. 194.

rather than surrender, she retreated from that faceless presence, but she retreated without turning away from his (or His) presence and her need. Backing away with an outstretched hand, she wanted only the pressure of that other hand. There must be a correspondence between herself, her experience, and an ultimate reality—for she felt it at times. But how to verify it, how to conceive it, how to formulate it except in tropes which expressed the flickerings of consciousness? Lacking the vocabulary and structure of a metaphysic, lodged in the fastness of the self and the tightness of the poetry, separate and detached like Whitman's patient spider, she cast forth "filament, filament, filament" out of herself—but in a world far more constricted than the circumference of Whitman's reach. For this reason the pressures of her tiny poems, probing in and probing out, express—more than *Walden* or *Leaves of Grass*—the crucial struggle within the American sensibility. In the perspective of history Dickinson is the pivotal point in the tension between Edwards' perception of types and Stevens' elaboration of tropes.

Hers was the individual consciousness aspiring to absolute vision on fitful wings as it dove into the funneling abyss of the self. And it is precisely in this image of a bird's simultaneous ascent and descent that Hart Crane hailed Emily Dickinson in *The Bridge*,* which is his own heroic effort to project absolute vision from personal vision:

> So must we from the hawk's far stemming view,
> Must we descend as worm's eye to construe
> Our love of all we touch, and take it to the Gate
> As humble as a guest who knows himself too late,
> His news already told? Yes, while the heart is wrung,
> Arise — yes, take this sheaf of dust upon your tongue!
> In one last angelus lift throbbing throat —
> Listen, transmuting silence with that stilly note

* *Collected Poems* (New York: Liveright, 1930), pp. 47–48.

Of pain that Emily, that Isadora knew! *
While high from dim elm-chancels hung with dew,
That triple-noted clause of moonlight —
Yes, whip-poor-will, unhusks the heart of fright,
Breaks us and saves, yes, breaks the heart, yet yields
That patience that is armour and that shields
Love from despair — when love foresees the end —
Leaf after autumnal leaf
> break off,
>> descend —
>>> descend —

The spinning rhetoric is Crane's, but how appropriate for Emily Dickinson is the poet's image that in our aspiration we transcend our limits, while an outpouring from above sustains us in our downward course. For others, the "natural Sabbath" of the nineteenth century became the naturalistic "Sunday Morning" of the twentieth, and Wallace Stevens, in his poem of that name, ended with a stoic acceptance of the bird's flight and fall:

> And, in the isolation of the sky,
> At evening, casual flocks of pigeons make
> Ambiguous undulations as they sink,
> Downward to darkness, on extended wings.**

2

The gradual course of Emily Dickinson's withdrawal, traced in the biographies and most minutely in Mr. Leyda's chronicle of her *Years and Hours*, is familiar enough not to need detailed narration here. The more elusive question is why she withdrew. Emily made several poignant references to an illustration in *Harper's* (the issue of June 1851, reproduced in Leyda I 201)

---

* This section of *The Bridge*, "Quaker Hill," is prefaced by two epigraphs: one from Isadora Duncan ("I see only the ideal. But no ideals have ever been fully successful on this earth"), and one from Emily Dickinson ("The gentian weaves her fringes/ The maple's loom is red").
** From *Collected Poems* (New York: Alfred A. Knopf, 1955), p. 70.

which is entitled "Tired of the World." A concerned grand-
mother asks a wistful child, "Why, what's the matter with my
Pet?" The child answers, hand pressed to mouth: "Why, Grand-
ma, after giving the subject every consideration, I have come to
the conclusion that — the World is Hollow, and my Doll is
stuffed with Sawdust, so — I — should — like — if you please, to
be a Nun?" [9] Studies of Emily Dickinson have already made
much — too much, in fact — of her trembling rejection of a false
and hollow world. As a matter of fact, for all the truth of that
point, the world was often not too insubstantial for her but too
substantial, and Emily Dickinson would have known exactly
what Thoreau feared when he wrote in *The Maine Woods*:

> I stand in awe of my body, this matter to which I am bound has
> become so strange to me . . . Think of our life in Nature, — daily
> to be shown matter, to come in contact with it — rocks, trees, wind on
> our cheeks! the *solid* earth! the *actual* world! the *common sense!*
> *Contact! Contact! Who* are we? *Where* are we?

Behind withdrawal, then, lay a complicated impulse, and Emerson's words of 1842 afford insight into the motive of those writers
whose "optative mood" set them apart from their fellows:

> They are lonely; the spirit of their writing and conversation is
> lonely; they repel influences; they shun general society; they incline
> to shut themselves in their chamber in the house, to live in the coun-
> try rather than in the town, and to find their tasks and amusements
> in solitude . . . this part is chosen both from temperament and from
> principle; with some unwillingness, too, and as a choice of the less
> of two evils; for . . . they have even more than others a great
> wish to be loved.[10]

Having withdrawn from the great world into her little village,
Emily Dickinson called herself "Amherst" (as she designated
Wadsworth "my Philadelphia" and Judge Lord "our sweet
Salem" [11]). She sometimes commented on the events of the day,
but the tenor of her remarks [12] indicates how far removed she was

from the world beyond the Berkshires.* Even in Amherst she felt the difference; to her brother she confided: "The Newmans seem very pleasant, but they are not *like us*. What makes a few of us so different from others? It's a question I often ask myself"; "I think we miss each other more every day that we grow older, for we're all unlike most everyone, and are therefore more dependent on each other for delight." From Amherst she sought shelter in her home: "Home is a holy thing — nothing of doubt or distrust can enter it's blessed portals . . ."; "They say that 'home is where the heart is.' I think it is where the *house* is, and adjacent buildings"; "Home is the definition of God." Yet so individualistic was the Dickinson "difference" that in the end each member of the family was isolated from the rest, and Emily had to conclude at last: "It is essential to the sanity of mankind that each one should think the other crazy . . ."[13]; and madness, which might mean genius ("a Divine Insanity"), is a tormenting preoccupation in the letters and poems. Was she mad or were the others mad? In self-defense she was compelled to say to Mrs. Holland: "Pardon my sanity . . . in a world *in*sane . . ."[14]

Consequently it was not so much a matter of taking her stand in Amherst as Thoreau did at Walden but rather one of retreating behind the façade of Amherst and home into the private self. When she wrote, "This is my letter to the World / That never wrote to Me," she was stating at least half the truth — namely, that the relationship which she desired between herself and the world was the occasional (but regular), remote (but direct) communication of epistolary correspondence. It is not surprising that her letters are much like her poems in texture and tech-

---

* Consider, for example, this remark about the Civil War (even after she had lost a friend that year in battle): "A Soldier called — a Morning ago, and asked for a Nosegay, to take to Battle. I suppose he thought we kept an Aquarium" (L II 416). Or this casual remark after Jay Cooke's bankruptcy had precipitated one of America's worst financial panics: "I should feel it my duty to lay my 'net' on the national altar, would it appease finance, but as Jay Cooke can't wear it, I suppose I won't" (L II 515).

nique, in movement and imagery, or that, generally speaking, the years which produced fewer poems produced more letters, and vice versa. In a letter she could be intensely (if obliquely) revealing without being intensely personal. Twice, in 1869 and 1882, she repeated that a "Letter always feels to me like immortality because it is the mind alone without corporeal friend" [15]; and since a letter was "spiritual converse,"

> The Way I read a Letter's — this —
> 'Tis first — I lock the Door —
> And push it with my fingers — next —
> For transport it be sure —
>
> And then I go the furthest off
> To counteract a knock —
> Then draw my little Letter forth
> And slowly pick the lock — (P 636, II.489)

Through letters she could cultivate close friendships and still keep them as distant as she wished; she could pick and choose her friends and yet hold them off by controlling the timing, the direction, and the tone of the epistolary proceedings. In this odd situation Higginson was driven to express his bafflement:

I have the greatest desire to see you, always feeling that perhaps if I could once take you by the hand I might be something to you; but till then you only enshroud yourself in this fiery mist & I cannot reach you, but only rejoice in the rare sparkles of light . . . I think if I could once see you & know that you are real, I might fare better. [16]

But after an interview he knew that he had not touched her and could not touch her, and that he was no more to her than before:

The impression undoubtedly made on me was that of an excess of tension, and of an abnormal life . . . Certainly I would have been most glad to bring it down to the level of simple truth and everyday companionship . . . an instinct told me that the slightest attempt at direct cross-examination would make her withdraw into her shell;

I could only sit still and watch, as one does in the woods; I must name my bird without a gun, as recommended by Emerson.[17]

The result was, as Emily must have realized and intended, that he could never quite name the bird. In the spirit of Thoreau's ideal, in which friendship precluded contact, she could say:

> So We must meet apart —
> You there — I — here —
> With just the Door ajar   (P 640, II.493)

Or even:

> We shun because we prize her Face
> Lest sight's ineffable disgrace
> Our Adoration stain   (P 1429, III.991)

Idealized sentiment, however, did not really explain her fastidiousness any more than Thoreau's words completely explained his.

Although Emily Dickinson did not know the word "mask" in our psychological and literary sense, she spoke of "Ourself behind ourself, concealed." In her fourth letter to Higginson she wanted to make sure that the mask was clearly visible: "When I state myself, as the Representative of the Verse — it does not mean — me — but a supposed person"; not the person whom one might meet as Emily Dickinson, but another "me," partly an expression of, partly a creation of, consciousness. In a mood of fanciful exuberance or coquetry she might sign her letters "Emilie"; as a reminder of her status as artist she might sign "Dickinson." Emily Fowler Ford remembered that when they were girls, Emily "once asked me, if it did not make me shiver to hear a great many people talk, they took [']all the clothes off their souls'"; and in 1884 the poet wrote retrospectively: "In all the circumference of Expression, those guileless words of Adam and Eve never were surpassed, 'I was afraid and hid Myself.'" Therefore, since she "would as soon undress in public, as to give my poems to the world," she hid even the poetic mask from notice and made a few select people her "little *World*" of readers.[18] In time, when she was safely gone, posterity would render that other "supposed" Emily Dickinson immortal acclaim.*

Her life in retirement was made possible only by those — family, friends, neighbors, and visitors — who supported her in the ways of her "remarkable personality." Her vagaries seemed the eccentricities which might be expected of a genius — certainly to be understood and allowed, perhaps to be encouraged, and rather to be enjoyed as a vicarious experience of the bizarre. And certainly there were many things that required toleration: her odd appearance; her white dresses; her occasional refusal to come downstairs to meet even close friends; her flurried flights from the room or from the garden at the approach of outsiders; her listening to music from the next room; her appointments to meet people "at the foot of the back stairs by moonlight alone"; her conversations from behind a door that stood ajar to screen her; her baskets of freshly baked sweets lowered to the neighborhood children by a pulley outside her window; her offering a guest the odd choice of a glass of wine or a rose; her ghostly appearances at social gatherings in the house (infrequent as such appearances were, until finally discontinued) when, having awaited "a moment when conversation lagged a little, she would sweep in, clad in immaculate white, pass through the rooms, silently courtseying and saluting right and left, and sweep out again"; her insistence even in her last illness that the only examination permitted the doctor was to observe her as she walked

* She wrote to Higginson: "If fame belonged to me, I could not escape her — and if she did not, the longest day would pass me on the chase — and the approbation of my Dog, would forsake me — then — My Barefoot — Rank is better —" (L II 408). And to Sue: "Could I make you and Austin — proud — sometime — a great way off — 'twould give me taller feet —" (L II 380). She was quoted as having said: "I have a horror of death; the dead are so soon forgotten. But when I die, they'll have to remember me" (Leyda II 481).

by an open door while he remained seated in the next room.[19] It was fortunate for her that others were compassionate enough or curious enough to humor her eccentricities.

Yet, in another sense, were they not also playing directly into her hands? Were they not behaving just as she wanted them to behave — sympathetic but remote, unapproaching but respectful of her genius? In this case, might not her peculiarities of manner be attributed not just to her fragile and ethereal sensibility but equally to a deliberately conceived, wilfully performed role? If people were held off, they could not make the myriad and constant demands of time and service which the Victorian spinster was expected to render without hesitation. In necessary self-defense the artist "Dickinson" executed an ingenious performance of the erratic "Emilie" and carried it off with unimpeachable success, in large part because the role came so naturally to her. The line between person and persona cannot be sharply drawn, but the distinction is important. The point is not that she was not eccentric but that she was exploiting her eccentricity (to some extent at least) for her own ends. She was adapting the exigencies of her temperament to the needs of her situation to construct a mask, which she then ruthlessly imposed on herself and ruthlessly thrust at others — a mask as calculated as Gabriel Rossetti's or Oscar Wilde's or Lionel Johnson's.

3

The association of Emily Dickinson with the English aesthetes and "decadents" is by no means gratuitous. Despite the differences in circumstance and character, they are all, behind their masks, poets in withdrawal. In England something had happened to the poetic imagination between Wordsworth's naturalism and Keats' positing of life (for all his talk of "negative capability") as the exploration of the chambers of the mind.

Keats was no aesthete, but aesthetes took what they wanted from him to explain their exquisite impressionism. From his seclusion at Oxford, Walter Pater spoke to and for many:

If we continue to dwell in thought on this world, not of objects in the solidity with which language invests them, but of impressions unstable, flickering, inconsistent, which burn and are extinguished with our consciousness of them, it [the consciousness of the observer] contracts still further; the whole scope of observation is dwarfed to the narrow chamber of the individual mind. Experience, already reduced to a swarm of impressions, is ringed round for each of us by that thick wall of personality through which no real voice has ever pierced on its way to us, or from us to that which we can only conjecture to be without. Every one of those impressions is the impression of the individual in his isolation, each mind keeping as a solitary prisoner its own dream of a world.[20]

The thick wall which chambered the individual in the void became for Oscar Wilde, literally and metaphorically, a terrifying cell: "I know that on the day of my release [from Reading Gaol] I shall be merely passing from one prison to another . . ."; since each man can know only "that world which is within" him, "one merely wanders round and round within the circle of one's own personality."[21]

To escape the stifling trap and breathe the open air, Gerard Manley Hopkins insisted upon a different definition of the circle:

Whatever can with truth be called a self . . . is not a mere centre or point of reference for consciousness or action attributed to it, everything else, all that it is conscious of or acts on being its object only and outside it. Part of this world of objects, this object-world, is also part of the very self in question . . . If the centre of reference spoken of has concentric circles round it, one of these, the inmost, say, is its own, is óf it, the rest are tó it only.

In other words, "I" cannot truly be myself unless I am related to independently existing objects. They exist for me in my perception of them, and thereby they modify and are assimilated by my consciousness. But this is not the perception of a private "dream of a world"; the objects are not of me but to me. The beholder and the beheld are separate but individually related, vitally conjoined. "A self then," continued Hopkins, "will consist of a centre *and* a surrounding area or circumference, of a point of reference *and* a belonging field," [22] set out from the center but set within its field of activity. Hopkins had thus worked his way back to the essential distinction and connection between the subject and the object, which his tutor Pater found himself incapable of making. "Inscape" and "instress" were Hopkins' terms to characterize the intensity which man's experience can reach: the inexplicable union of interacting but distinct beings. Not only do circles have diameter and expanding circumference; sometimes centers converge and coincide.

In America the drift toward egocentricity can be traced in the increasing tendency of the imagination to conceive experience in tropes rather than types. The words of Emerson which come ringing down the decades are not "Nature is the symbol of spirit," but rather "Nothing is at last sacred but the integrity of your own mind." For Emerson the two statements were synonymous: one moved in and out of the mind simultaneously, and thereby the self-reliant individual transcended the ego coiled back, tail in mouth, feeding on itself. In the twentieth century Eliot moved dramatically from "each in his prison / Thinking of the key," to freedom at "the still point of the turning world." In the process, however, Eliot returned, intellectually and spiritually, to a conception of reality which is antecedent to Emerson, to Edwards even, and even to New England Puritanism; and so his late personal-impersonal verse finds its closest analogue in American literature in the work of Edward Taylor, the Puritan-metaphysical poet. For all Eliot's influence, his religious course ran counter to the direction of the age. Most modern poets have sought to achieve and maintain within themselves, but without Emerson's transcendentalism, the sacred integrity of the mind: a directness of intention and incisiveness of vision in which they could strive to comprehend (in both senses: to take in and to understand) what they saw and felt. Through the concentration and rigor with which consciousness operates upon experience, poets as different as Hart Crane and William Carlos Williams have established their individual circumferences in what Williams called "an agony of self-realization / bound into a whole / by that which surrounds us." * The dimensions and variety of Robert Lowell's poetry encompass all his fears of paralysis in the "blear-eyed ego": "The Quaker Graveyard in Nantucket" is one of the sublime poems of American literature, and even the autobiographical voice of *Life Studies* has involved itself in the more public concerns of *For the Union Dead.* John Berryman's *Dream Songs* include both private torment and bold social statement, as the poet moves in and out and around the persona "Henry." The impact which the "beat" movement registered on the contemporary poetic consciousness was its thrust to open out again to an organic sense of things. Allen Ginsberg may sound at times like Whitman howling in hell, but part of the power of Ginsberg's oratory proceeds from his determination to face his hell and then break out of it. The whole impulse of the poetry of Brother Antoninus (William Everson) is the painful definition of the self within an encircling absolute: first, within the sweep of a life force which animates nature pantheistically (as Jeffers had said) and man sexually (as Henry Miller had said); and in the later poems within the mystery of the Incarnation. Modern poetry displays a remarkable diversity of viewpoints and techniques; in each case, however, the poet is seeking, in his own way and on his own terms, to make himself

* *The Desert Music and Other Poems* (New York: Random House, 1954), p. 73.

the center of an area of reference and (hopefully) of clarity, lest the ego lock on itself in the void.

4

Emily Dickinson's physical seclusion was a sign of her emotional and psychological withdrawal; but in the spirit of Thoreau's boast that he had "travelled a good deal in Concord," she proclaimed "Area — no test of depth," and manifested the universality of her narrow experience by weaving the names of foreign and faraway places into her tight verses.[23] Within her chosen and preappointed limits she made poems which are astonishing for their range and intensity and for their experiments in language — in short, for their enactment of the individual drama of consciousness. Thoreau could almost have had her in mind when he wrote

How much is there in simply seeing! . . . The woman who sits in the house and *sees* is a match for a stirring captain. Those still, piercing eyes, as faithfully exercised on their talent, will keep her even with Alexander or Shakespeare. They may go to Asia with parade, or to fairyland, but not beyond her ray.[24]

Nevertheless, the imposition of limits would necessarily mean a restriction of possibilities. Even if she was, as she claimed, "by birth a Bachelor," or, like Thoreau, could live and write only as "the bachelor of thought and Nature," still bachelorhood meant the forfeit of vast areas of experience. Thoreau could write that it is "mere sentimentality that lies abed by day and thinks itself white, far from the tan and callus of experience," and could think that he had known the tan and callus. But when Emerson observed that for Thoreau there were "no temptations to fight against, — no appetites, no passions, no taste for elegant trifles," the compliment was, even in Emerson's mind, questionable.[25]

Since for Emily Dickinson there were greater temptations and passions and appetites to fight against, suppression meant a more costly sacrifice.

She recognized the struggle clearly and knew precisely what she was doing:

> We shun it ere it comes,
> Afraid of Joy,
> Then sue it to delay
> And lest it fly,
> Beguile it more and more —
>
> (P 1580, III.1088)

Like Isabel Archer in *Portrait of a Lady*, Emily Dickinson wanted to know and see — but untouched at a safe distance. And she deserves credit for recognizing and accepting the consequences of keeping her distance: in her world, as she said, "there is not so much Life as *talk* of Life, as a general thing." [26]

The exciting thing about Emily Dickinson's poems and letters is that although the centrifugal movement out from consciousness was less forceful than the centripetal movement into consciousness, both impulses were still active in her, still tugging against one another, still seeking equilibrium. She knew that "each life converges to some Centre." [27] The question was where the center — unknown and "scarcely embodied to itself" — lies. Is the goal within our individuality? This would compel us to absorb externals into the fullest cultivation of consciousness. Or is the goal without? This would compel us to seek ourselves in a transcendent reality. Edwards, Emerson, and Eliot would have told her that loss of self and fullness of self were finally the same. But, in the uncertainty of a quest as religious as theirs, centers did not consistently converge, and Emily Dickinson could only search herself and as much of the world as she could manage. In answer to his question "what to make of a diminished thing," Frost summed up the possibility:

But the comfort is
In the covenant
We may get control
If not of the whole
Of at least some part
Where not too immense,
So by craft or art
We can give the part
Wholeness in a sense.*

There is perhaps no better way to conclude than to come full circle back to the passage from an early letter cited in the first chapter as the rubric or text for this consideration of Emily Dickinson's mind and art. Here again, in many of the images which would become familiar emblems throughout the poems and letters — the child, the virgin-bride, the wife, the flower, the dewy morning, the sun, the burning noon, the master — is the paradoxical dilemma of the double consciousness, spiraling out and spiraling back on itself:

You and I have been strangely silent upon this subject, Susie, we have often touched upon it, and as quickly fled away, as children shut their eyes when the sun is too bright for them. I have always hoped to know if you had no dear fancy, illumining all your life, no one of whom you murmured in the faithful ear of night — and at whose side in fancy, you walked the livelong day; and when you come home, Susie, we must speak of these things. How dull our lives must seem to the bride, and the plighted maiden, whose days are fed with gold, and who gathers pearls every evening; but to the *wife*, Susie, sometimes the *wife forgotten*, our lives perhaps seem dearer than all the others in the world; you have seen flowers at morning, *satisfied* with the dew, and those same sweet flowers at noon with their heads bowed in anguish before the mighty sun; think you these thirsty blossoms will *now* need nought but — *dew*? No, they will cry for sunlight, and pine for the burning noon, tho' it scorches

* Lines from "Kitty Hawk," from *In the Clearing* (New York, 1962) by Robert Frost. Copyright © 1956, 1962 by Robert Frost. Reprinted by permission of Holt, Rinehart and Winston, Inc.

174

them, scathes them; they have got through with peace — they know that the man of noon, is *mightier* than the morning and their life is henceforth to him. Oh, Susie, it is dangerous, and it is all too dear, these simple, trusting spirits, and the spirits mightier, which we cannot resist! It does so rend me, Susie, the thought of it when it comes, that I tremble lest at sometime I, too, am yielded up. Susie, you will forgive my amatory strain — it has been a very long one, and if this saucy page did not here bind and fetter me, I might have had no end.[28]

As a matter of fact, she did not have an end there; she had a lifetime to pursue and record the ramifications of the paradox. From the seclusion of home she worked out her bold and far-reaching design. To Higginson she set forth without equivocation her singular concern as a poet: "Perhaps you smile at me. I could not stop for that — My Business is Circumference." So from within the tightening circle — the circle tightening around herself by choice and despite choice, or, as Emerson said, "both from temperament and from principle; with some unwillingness, too"[29] — she negotiated with man, God, nature, and language to carry on the business of circumference.

BIBLIOGRAPHY

NOTES

INDEX

SELECTED BIBLIOGRAPHY

The authoritative editions of Emily Dickinson's writings are: *The Poems of Emily Dickinson*, ed. Thomas H. Johnson. Cambridge, Mass.: The Belknap Press of Harvard University Press, 1955; and *The Letters of Emily Dickinson*, ed. Thomas H. Johnson and Theodora Ward. Cambridge, Mass.: The Belknap Press of Harvard University Press, 1958. There is also a one-volume *Complete Poems*, edited by Mr. Johnson with his transcription of the texts but without variants or manuscript notes (Boston: Little, Brown & Co., 1960).

The following are the most useful and stimulating scholarly biographies:

Chase, Richard. *Emily Dickinson*. New York: William Sloane Associates, 1951.

Johnson, Thomas H. *Emily Dickinson: An Interpretive Biography*. Cambridge, Mass.: The Belknap Press of Harvard University Press, 1955.

Whicher, George Frisbie. *This Was a Poet: A Critical Biography of Emily Dickinson*. New York: Charles Scribners' Sons, 1939.

There is also a superb source book which compiles in two volumes a chronological account of Emily Dickinson and her milieu from newspapers, magazines, and so forth, as well as from the writings of the poet, her family, and her friends: *The Years and Hours of Emily Dickinson*, ed. Jay Leyda. New Haven: Yale University Press, 1960.

The following are other helpful and illuminating writings, biographical or critical, concerning Emily Dickinson:

Anderson, Charles R. *Emily Dickinson's Poetry: Stairway of Surprise*. New York: Holt, Rinehart, & Winston, 1960.

Bingham, Millicent Todd. *Ancestors' Brocades: The Literary Debut of Emily Dickinson*. New York: Harper & Bros., 1945.

—— *Emily Dickinson: A Revelation*. New York: Harper & Bros., 1954.

—— *Emily Dickinson's Home: Letters of Edward Dickinson and His Family with Documentation and Comment*. New York: Harper & Bros., 1955.

Blackmur, R. P. "Emily Dickinson: Notes in Prejudice and Fact," in *The Experience of Greatness*. New York: Arrow Editions, 1940.

MacLeish, Archibald. "The Private World: Poems of Emily Dickinson," in *Poetry and Experience*. Boston, Mass.: Houghton Mifflin Co., 1961.

————, Louise Bogan, and Richard Wilbur. *Emily Dickinson: Three Views*. Amherst: Amherst College Press, 1960.

Matthiessen, F. O. "The Problem of the Private Poet," in *Kenyon Review*, 7:584–597 (1945).

Tate, Allen. "Emily Dickinson," in *Reactionary Essays on Poetry and Ideas*. New York: Charles Scribners' Sons, 1936.

Winters, Yvor. "Emily Dickinson and the Limits of Judgment," in *Maule's Curse: Seven Studies in the History of American Obscurantism*. Norfolk, Conn.: New Directions, 1938.

The following are two anthologies of critical essays on Emily Dickinson:

Emily Dickinson: A Collection of Critical Essays, ed. Richard B. Sewall, in the Twentieth-Century Views Series. Englewood Cliffs, N. J.: Prentiss-Hall Inc., 1963.

The Recognition of Emily Dickinson: Selected Criticism Since 1890. Ann Arbor: University of Michigan Press, 1964.

Other books on Emily Dickinson, which are occasionally useful, are:

Bianchi, Martha Dickinson. *Emily Dickinson Face to Face: Unpublished Letters with Notes and Reminiscences by Her Niece*. Boston: Houghton Mifflin Co., 1932.

———— *The Life and Letters of Emily Dickinson*. Boston: Houghton Mifflin Co., 1924.

Griffith, Clark. *The Long Shadow: Emily Dickinson's Tragic Poetry*. Princeton, N. J.: Princeton University Press, 1964.

Jenkins, MacGregor. *Emily Dickinson: Friend and Neighbor*. Boston: Little, Brown & Co., 1930.

Patterson, Rebecca. *The Riddle of Emily Dickinson*. Boston: Houghton Mifflin Co., 1951.

Pollitt, Josephine. *Emily Dickinson: The Human Background of Her Poetry*. New York: Harper & Bros., 1930.

Power, Sister Mary James. *In the Name of the Bee: The Significance of Emily Dickinson*. New York: Sheed & Ward, 1943.

Taggard, Genevieve. *The Life and Mind of Emily Dickinson*. New York: Alfred A. Knopf, 1930.

Ward, Theodora. *The Capsule of the Mind: Chapters in the Life of Emily Dickinson*. Cambridge, Mass.: The Belknap Press of Harvard University Press, 1961.

Wells, Henry Willis. *Introduction to Emily Dickinson*. Chicago: Hendricks House, 1947.

NOTES

CHAPTER I: The Problem of the One and the Two

1. *The Letters of Emily Dickinson*, ed. Thomas H. Johnson and Theodora Ward (Cambridge, Mass., 1958), I, 209–210. Henceforth in notes the Johnson edition of the *Letters* will be indicated by the capital letter L, followed by the volume and pages of the references, as in: L I 209–210.

2. L II 341.

CHAPTER II: Preceptors

1. L II 569.

2. Quoted in Millicent Todd Bingham, *Emily Dickinson's Home: Letters of Edward Dickinson and His Family* (New York, 1955), p. 407. Henceforth this book will be referred to as *Home*, followed by the page numbers.

3. Jay Leyda, *The Years and Hours of Emily Dickinson* (New Haven, 1960), II, 218. Henceforth this work will be referred to as Leyda, followed by the volume and page numbers, as in: Leyda II 218.

4. Leyda II 179, 203.

5. The first passage is quoted in Richard Chase, *Emily Dickinson* (William Sloane Associates, 1951), p. 13; the second, in Leyda I 4.

6. Leyda I 4.

7. *Home*, p. 17; MacGregor Jenkins, *Emily Dickinson: Friend and Neighbor* (Boston, 1930), p. 23; L II 245.

8. Leyda I 3.

9. Leyda I 14, 41; Jenkins, p. 23; L I 113; L II 526, 542.

10. L II 528; Leyda I 248; L I 269, 190; L II 486, 531.

11. L II 439; L III 663; L I 119; L I 231.

12. L II 337; L III 716.

13. L I 161; Leyda I 240; L I 111.

14. L I 233.

15. Leyda II 224; *Home*, p. 27; Leyda I 178.

16. L I 111; L II 537.

17. Leyda II 478.
18. L I 77; L II 404, 473; L I 237, 161; L II 475; L I 243.
19. L I 111, 190, 185–186.
20. Leyda II 478–479; Leyda I 177–178; Leyda II 231.
21. L I 304.
22. L I 282; L I 283; L III 727; L I 84; L II 408.
23. See L I 174, 180, 214, 219, 242, 246–247, 253, 260, 266, 279, 286, 290, 294–295, 300–305.
24. Leyda I 283, 271, 312, 311; L I 246, 266, 247, 305, 286.
25. L I 173, 148, 470.
26. L I 121.
27. L I 231; Leyda II 224; Leyda I 328; L II 475, 508, 555; Leyda II 482; L I 213. The Poem can be found in *The Poems of Emily Dickinson*, ed. Thomas H. Johnson (Cambridge, Mass., 1955), II, 649. Henceforth references to the poems will be to this edition; the notes will indicate after the letter P the number of the poem and the volume and page numbers, as in P874 II 649.
28. L II 528.
29. L II 452.
30. L II 559. For elegies of her father, see P1300 III 905, P1312 III 909, P1325 III 916, P1328 III 918, P1334 III 922, P1342 III 927, P1346 III 929–930, P1352 III 933, P1365 III 943, P1393 III 960.
31. L I 111–112.
32. *Home*, p. 375.
33. L III 738, 742, 744, 900–901.
34. L III 738, 753, 737.
35. P800 II 605.
36. P485 I 371.
37. L II 374.
38. L II 392.
39. Leyda II 102.
40. *Home*, p. 368.
41. Leyda I 181.
42. *Home*, p. 368.
43. *Home*, p. 369; L III 745, 738, 744. In L III 745 a quatrain associates Wadsworth's death and resurrection directly with Christ's, thus reasserting the identity or correspondence of the "Masters."
44. L II 409, 460.
45. L II 404.
46. Leyda II 79.
47. Leyda II 148, 123, 138, 168.
48. Leyda II 127; L II 404; Leyda II 153.
49. L II 409.

50. Leyda II 213.
51. L III 861, 728, 747, 727.
52. L II 617.
53. Leyda II 475.
54. L II 563.

CHAPTER III: The Mind against Itself

1. L I 27.
2. L I 30, 38.
3. P1357 III 938.
4. Leyda I 123, 136.
5. Leyda I 135–136; L I 58, 60; Leyda I 137; L I 67.
6. L I 98–99.
7. L I 104; L III 922, 882. For passages in which she talks of omitting church services, see L I 140, 181, 187, 251; L II 327, 358.
8. L III 923; P21 I 22; L II 480, 390.
9. For metaphors of voyage, harbors, drowning, and shipwreck, see P30 I 28; P76 I 61; P78 I 63; P159 I 115; P201 I 143; P226 I 162; P249 I 179; P506 II 388; P695 II 536; P739 II 563; P808 II 610; P825 II 625–626; P847 II 638; P872 II 648–649; P879 II 652; P881 II 653; P923 II 674; P944 II 685–686; P1123 II 788–789; P1136 II 797–798; P1137 II 799; P1217 III 848–849; P1234 III 858–859; P1263 III 879–880; P1264 III 880; P1409 III 978; P1425 III 988–989; P1749 III 1175. See also L II 503; L III 860, 890, 896.
10. L II 479.
11. L II 364; P377 I 300; L II 463.
12. P1724 III 1162; P532 II 409; P1663 III 1134; P364 I 289; L II 543; P1400 III 970–971; P1624 III 1114.
13. L III 916; P623 II 480; P240 I 173; L I 201–202; P576 II 440; L II 376; P724 II 554; P376 I 299. For references to God as Jehovah, see P1076 II 761; P116 I 85; P455 I 351; P476 I 365; P626 II 481; P982 II 708; P1748 III 1174; L II 528, 617; L III 880.
14. P1730 III 1165; P914 II 670; P49 I 38.
15. L III 716; P564 II 431; P338 I 270; P672 II 519.
16. P1317 III 911; P536 II 413; P476 I 365–366; P178 I 130.
17. "Personal Narrative" in *Jonathan Edwards*, ed. Clarence H. Faust & Thomas H. Johnson (New York, 1935), pp. 58–59.
18. P900 II 662; P1719 III 1159; L II 353; P116 I 85; P59 I 44; L III 705, 898, 903.
19. There are interesting biographical parallels between Margaret Fuller and Emily Dickinson: the awesome and possessive father; the

sense of difference, the sensitivity and superiority; the inherited New England temperament at odds with the insurgent Romantic spirit; the craving for love (which became with Margaret a kind of psychological assault on her intellectual associates); the resistance to a reciprocal human relationship. Margaret, however, lacked the art which served Emily as a means of releasing and controlling, of experiencing and expressing — in short, as a way of life. Margaret was too intelligent and too honest to tell herself that she could be a first-rate, or even perhaps a second-rate, artist. So, while Emily learned to "contemplate / Vesuvius at Home" (P1705 III 1153), the turmoil in Margaret boiled to the surface and spilled over, driving her from place to place, from person to person, from project to project. Where Emily's life was alarmingly private, Margaret's was alarmingly public, and not infrequently was the talk of the discountenanced town. Anne Bradstreet had been, without much difficulty, a Puritan, a poet, a wife, and a mother; but then Anne Bradstreet was long dead, and New England was much changed when Margaret and Emily were starting from much the same point and following their divergent paths. Still, divergent though their paths were, neither woman was more alive than when she took up her pen in secret: Emily to fashion her verses and letters, Margaret to flood the pages of her correspondence and her private journal.

20. P1617 III 1110.

21. Leyda II 477; L I 99, 306, 88.

22. P407 I 317; P1238 III 861.

23. L II 349; L III 700.

24. L II 359.

25. L II 505; P1357 III 938; P1270 III 884.

26. See, for example, L II 346; P970 II 702.

27. See L II 485; L III 728.

28. L III 756, 667; P503 II 386; P403 I 315; L III 711; P597 II 458; L III 711.

29. L III 837; L II 502–503.

30. L III 896, 703; L I 129; L III 684, 871, 690, 754. Other instances of the adaptation of Scripture are: L I 175, 183, 215; L II 329, 340, 541; L III 670.

31. P1439 III 999; L I 217; P1545 III 1066; P1601 III 1102–1103; P1751 III 1176; L III 753; L II 524–525; L III 835; L II 346; L III 861; L II 609; L II 339; L I 94.

32. P1499 III 1034–1035; P501 II 384–385; P1017 II 728; P866 II 655; P860 II 643; P1195 III 833; L II 481, 480; P1603 III 1103–1104.

33. L III 861; L II 559; P1157 III 1072; L III 731, 750, 779, 803; P1597 III 1100; L III 905.

34. For poems about her death, her corpse, her funeral, see, for example, P146 I 104–105; P445 I 344–345; P449 I 347; P465 I 358; P712 II 546; P1026 II 731; P1037 II 735.

35. L II 358.

CHAPTER IV: Seeing New Englandly

1. L II 620; L III 866, 798.

2. See Perry Miller, *The New England Mind: The Seventeenth Century* (Cambridge, Mass., 1954), pp. 7–8, 10–34.

3. See Perry Miller, "From Edwards to Emerson," in *Errand into the Wilderness* (Cambridge, Mass., 1956), pp. 184–203.

4. Perry Miller, *The New England Mind: From Colony to Province* (Cambridge, Mass., 1953), p. 69.

5. See Allen Tate, "Emily Dickinson," in *Reactionary Essays on Poetry and Ideas* (New York, 1936), pp. 3–26.

6. *Margaret Fuller: American Romantic*, ed. Perry Miller (New York, 1963), p. 58.

7. See George Frisbie Whicher, *This Was a Poet: A Critical Biography of Emily Dickinson* (New York, 1939), pp. 190ff.

8. *Ibid.*, p. 190.

9. *Ibid.*, pp. 39–40; Leyda I 150, 296, 331, 356; L III 713.

10. Cf. L II 539; L III 756, 775, 856, 882.

11. Leyda I 334, 351–352, 102, 309–310; L III 913, 928; *Home*, p. 572; L II 626, 627.

12. L II 455, 586; L III 692; Leyda II 141.

13. L I 92.

14. L I 3.

15. L I 13, 88.

16. L I 95.

17. L III 751.

18. L I 144, 181; L II 327–328; L I 235, 264; *Home*, p. 319; L I 272, 305–306.

19. See L I 117, 296.

20. L I 143, 148–149, 196; L II 330.

21. L III 911; L II 315, 594, 560.

22. L III 714, 928–929.

23. P985 II 711; P1732 III 1166; P959 II 695.

24. L I 167; L II 489; P1093 II 770.

25. P552 II 401; P664 II 511; P1660 III 1133.

26. L III 750–751; P73 I 58.

27. P945 II 687; P844 II 637; L III 880; P694 II 536.

28. "Natural History of Massachusetts," in *Excursions* (Boston, 1893), pp. 127–128.

29. P1462 III 1010; P349 I 279; P800 II 605; P1090 II 769.

30. L II 415.

31. P1039 II 736.

32. P184 I 134.

33. P1315 III 911; in addition, cf. P319 I 243–244; P1125 II 790; P1382 III 952.

34. Perry Miller, *The New England Mind: The Seventeenth Century*, p. 25.

35. Orestes A. Brownson, "New Views of Christianity, Society, and the Church" in *The Transcendentalists*, ed. Perry Miller (Cambridge, Mass., 1950), pp. 115–123.

36. Theodore Parker, "A Discourse of Matters Pertaining to Religion" in *The Transcendentalists*, pp. 316–324.

37. L II 329.

38. Cf., for example, P63 I 48; P65 I 50–51; P428 I 331–332; P977 II 706; P1024 II 730–731; P1043 II 738; P1228 III 854.

39. L II 329; P562 II 430; P239 I 172; P1684 III 1144; L II 579, 504.

40. P1012 II 726; L II 593, 592.

41. L II 424. For other comments on earth and heaven, see P418 I 325; P575 II 439; P1544 III 1065; L II 478, 550, 553, 594–595; L III 928.

42. P766 II 582; P783 II 591; L II 554; P1077 II 762; L II 333.

43. Leyda II 414. For other poems on nature as process, see P386 I 305; P1114 II 783; P1154 II 808; P1267 III 882; P1369 III 945; P1669 III 1137; P1756 III 1178; P1762 III 1181.

44. See, for example, P1067 II 751; P1142 II 801; P1349 III 932; P1422 III 986–987; P1434 III 994; P1741 III 1171.

45. L II 490; P1741 III 1171; P938 II 682; L III 848.

46. For poems on wind, see P315 I 238; P316 I 239–240; P416 I 323–324; P513 II 394–395; P516 II 396–397; P774 II 586–587; P945 II 687; P998 II 721; P1118 II 786–787; P1271 III 884; P1397 III 967; P1418 III 984; P1530 III 1055; P1656 III 1131.

47. P316 I 239; P416 I 323; P315 I 238; P1397 III 967; P998 II 721.

48. For poems on lightning, see P362 I 288; P393 I 309; P420 I 326; P480 I 368; P630 II 485; P824 II 624–625; P925 II 675; P974 II 704; P1129 II 792; P1173 II 819; P1247 III 866; P1468 III 1017; P1475 III 1021; P1581 III 1089; P1593 III 1098; P1660 III 1133.

49. P974 II 704; P1581 III 1089.

50. For poems referring to noon, see P63 I 48; P112 I 82; P197 I 216–217; P512 II 393–394; P575 II 439; P579 II 443; P638 II 490; P646 II 497; P673 II 520; P882 II 653; P916 II 671; P930 II 678; P931 II 679; P978 II 706; P1023 II 730; P1056 II 745; P1233 III 858; P1581 III 1089.

51. P624 II 480; P1056 II 745. For other poems referring to Eden or earth-heaven, see P24 I 24–25; P148 I 106; P374 I 298; P756 II 575–576; P839 II 635; L III 928.

52. P180 I 132. See also P249 I 179; P385 I 304–305; P503 II 386; P1657 III 1131–1132.

53. P1657 III 1131–1132; L II 454, 254, 508; P215 I 151.

54. L II 482; P18 I 21; P1209 III 841.

55. L III 683; P508 II 389–390; P473 I 363.

56. For references to grace in the poems, see P343 I 274; P359 I 286; P472 I 362; P569 II 434–435; P743 II 566; P744 II 586–587; P968 II 700–701; P1313 III 910. For references to revelation, see L II 424; P694 II 535–536. For references to renunciation, justification, and election, see P313 I 236–237; P322 I 249–250; P343 I 274–275; P528 II 405; P569 II 434; P745 II 568; P751 II 572. For references to Sacrament and miracles, see L I 207; L III 825; P74 I 59–60; P130 I 92–93; P495 II 379; P646 II 497; P1297 III 900. For other poems referring to Sacrament, see P383 I 303; P535 II 412; P751 II 572; P812 II 613; P1651 III 1129.

57. P1157 III 1131–1132; L III 699. See also P70 I 56; P788 II 594–595; P973 II 704; Leyda II 114, 377.

58. L II 539; L I 37; L II 504. See also L I 16, 66; L II 323, 354; P1178 III 822; P1437 III 995–996; P1530 III 1055; P1682 III 1143–1144; P1764 III 1182.

59. L I 130; P1498 III 1034; L III 843. For other poems referring to a momentous interview, whether with God, lover, or friend, see P247 I 177–178; P293 I 211–212; P296 I 215–216; P322 I 249–250; P410 I 319; P663 II 510–511; P768 II 583; P800 II 605; P902 II 663.

60. For poems about prospect and retrospect, see P379 I 300; P867 II 646; P1196 III 833; P1227 III 853–854; P1271 III 884; P1353 III 934; P1416 III 982–983; P1498 III 1034; P1742 III 1171; L II 452; L III 922.

61. L II 474; P1247 III 866.

62. P1585 III 1092; P1209 III 841; P488 I 372–373.

63. P1544 III 1065.

64. Emily Dickinson mentioned Edwards only twice: L I 121; P1522 III 1049.

65. P1545 III 1065–1066.

66. *The Complete Poems of Robert Frost* (New York, 1949), p. vi.

CHAPTER V: The Business of Circumference

1. P1323 III 915; P1695 III 1149; P822 II 622–623; L II 500.

2. P565 II 432; L II 551, 519; P1181 III 824; L III 715; P454 I 350; P1351 III 933; L II 483; P1295 III 898–899.

3. For imagery of exploration and discovery, see P669 II 516; P832 II 631; P905 II 665; P1354 III 935; L III 715.

4. "Of Modern Poetry," *Collected Poems* (New York, 1955), p. 240.

5. See "The Oversoul" in *Essays: First Series*.

6. For poems on consciousness, see P384 I 304; P642 II 494; P674 II 521; P750 II 571; P786 II 593; P787 II 594; P799 II 604–605; P815 II 616; P822 II 622–623; P826 II 626; P827 II 626; P832 II 631; P876 II 650; P894 II 659; P911 II 669; P978 II 706–707; P982 II 708–709; P1056 II 745; P1088 II 768; P1238 III 861; P1323 III 915; P1454 III 1006–1007. For consciousness as home, cf. L II 634.

7. W. H. Auden, "The Globe," in *The Dyer's Hand and Other Essays* (New York, 1962), p. 171.

8. For poems on the present moment, see P978 II 706–707; P1133 II 795; P1253 III 869; P1380 III 951; P1540 III 1061–1062.

9. For references to theater, show, and circus, see P184 I 134; P243 I 175–176; P290 I 209; P354 I 282–283; P531 II 408; P569 II 434–435; P595 II 456; P582 II 445; P627 II 482; P628 II 483; P658 II 507; P741 II 564–565; P794 II 600; P827 II 626; P936 II 681–682; P1206 III 838–839; P1349 III 932; P1482 III 1024–1025; P1501 III 1036; P1626 III 1115; P1644 III 1125; L II 495, 507, 524, 644; L III 753.

10. P1380 III 951.

11. For poems on the duality of experience, see P135 I 96; P384 I 304; P395 I 310; P459 I 354; P512 II 393–394; P571 II 436; P574 II 438; P627 II 482; P772 II 585; P1168 II 816; P1196 III 833; P1287 III 894; P1726 III 1163; P1774 III 1186.

12. P711 II 545–546; P807 II 610; P857 II 642; P1109 II 780–781.

13. P1133 II 795; P167 I 122; L III 921.

14. L II 404.

15. Jonathan Edwards, *Images or Shadows of Divine Things*, ed. Perry Miller, p. 126.

16. Robert Frost, "Kitty Hawk" in *In the Clearing* (New York, 1962), p. 48.

17. L I 305, 311; P1765 III 1183; P1648 III 1128. For the association of love with church, sacrament, and grace, see P322 I 249–250; P387 I 306; P491 I 374; P725 II 554–555; P833 II 631–632; P939 II 683; P1555 III 1071.

18. Leyda II 474.

19. L III 858, 862.

20. P528 II 405; P664 II 511; P303 I 225; P1248 III 866.

21. For poems on love, see the following numbers (the volume and page numbers are omitted here to save space): 31, 124, 190, 196, 199, 203, 205, 206, 208, 209, 211, 212, 213, 217, 232, 235, 236, 245, 247, 248, 249, 260, 261, 263, 267, 270, 271, 273, 275, 276, 293, 295, 296, 322, 336, 350, 366, 368, 387, 398, 410, 418, 438, 456, 498, 506, 549, 577, 587, 616, 622, 631, 640, 648, 663, 664, 704, 710, 715, 725, 738, 754, 768, 781, 788, 850, 869, 881, 939, 944, 961, 1042, 1059, 1125, 1132, 1189, 1231, 1260, 1449, 1476, 1507, 1548.

22. See P190 I 137; P203 I 144; P205 I 145; P236 I 170–171; P478 I 367; P573 II 437; P1230 III 856; P1743 III 1172.

23. See P260 I 186–187; P295 I 214; P322 I 249–250; P348 I 278; P405 I 316; P501 II 384–385; P506 II 388–389; P527 II 404–405; P544 II 417–418; P549 II 420; P553 II 423; P571 II 436; P573 II 437; P620 II 477; P725 II 554–555; P792 II 598; P1072 II 758; P1304 III 906–907; P1375 III 948; P1432 III 992; P1612 III 1108; P1735 III 1167; P1736 III 1168; P1737 III 1168–1169; L III 861.

24. Leyda I 111, 346; Leyda II 6; L II 325–327.

25. For sentimental-macabre poems on death, see P9 I 11–12; P141 I 100; P146 I 104–105; P150 I 107; P187 I 135–136; P344 I 275–276; P366 I 291–292; P369 I 294; P445 I 344–345; P509 II 390–391; P577 II 441–442; P586 II 448; P588 II 450; P598 II 459; P611 II 470; P616 II 473–474; P622 II 478–479; P640 II 492–493; P648 II 498–499; P715 II 548; P1026 II 731; P1037 II 735; P1061 II 748; P1100 II 773–774; P1759 III 1180.

26. For poems on death, see the following numbers (the volume and page numbers have been omitted here to save space): 71, 158, 171, 187, 255, 280, 281, 286, 287, 358, 360, 382, 389, 390, 391, 392, 408, 409, 414, 426, 432, 444, 457, 465, 468, 483, 519, 547, 552, 577, 590, 610, 611, 614, 619, 622, 665, 671, 692, 698, 712, 758, 795, 813, 814, 976, 981, 1026, 1065, 1078, 1100, 1135, 1149, 1188, 1230, 1272, 1300, 1312, 1325, 1328, 1334, 1342, 1346, 1352, 1365, 1378, 1384, 1393, 1445, 1478, 1490, 1492, 1523, 1525, 1527, 1605, 1674, 1686, 1691, 1692, 1701, 1703, 1716.

27. P573 II 437; P522 II 401; P394 I 309–310. For poems on death as king, suitor, and redeemer: see P98 I 76; P171 I 125–126; P235 I 170; P279 I 199; P465 I 358; P665 II 512; P712 II 546; P1053 II 743; P1123 II 788–789; P1445 III 1001.

28. L II 341; P1256 III 871; P970 II 702; P98 I 76; P1238 III 861; P171 I 125–126; P235 I 170.

29. P907 II 666; P809 II 611; L II 454; P1737 III 1168–1169; P1580 III 1188; P357 I 284; P817 II 618; P1496 III 1033; P171 I 125–126; P279 I 199; P665 II 512; P694 II 697–698; P1123 II 788–789;

P350 I 279; P464 I 358; P640 II 492–493; P648 II 498–499; P664 II 511; P788 II 594–595; P1260 III 875–876; P1492 III 1031; P1743 III 1172.

30. P463 I 357; P626 II 480–481; P781 II 590; P833 II 631–632; P907 II 666–667; P1001 II 723; P1231 III 857; P1305 III 907; P1737 III 1168–1169.

31. P917 II 671; P491 I 374; P809 II 611; P984 II 710; P1495 III 1032.

32. For references to immortality and consciousness, see, in addition to the previous citations, L I 264; L II 484, 576; P306 I 227–228; P1056 II 745; P1090 II 769.

33. For poems on birds, see P143 I 102–103; P1570 III 1082; P1600 III 1102; P1723 III 1161–1162; L I 75, 264, 284, 306–307; L II 336, 339, 411, 465, 618; Leyda II 480. For jewels, see P11 I 14; P245 I 176; P270 I 192; P299 I 218–219; P304 I 226; P320 I 245; P427 I 331; P466 I 359; P493 I 375; P693 II 535; P1108 II 780. For caterpillars and butterflies, see P129 I 92; P354 I 282–283; P397 I 311; P1099 II 772–773; P1244 III 864; P1387 III 956; Leyda II 258. For spots and freckles, see P163 I 119; P166 I 121–122; P209 I 147; P275 I 196; P401 I 314; P964 II 697–698; P1094 II 770; P1311 III 909; P1737 III 1168; see also L II 377, 383. For poems on white, see P221 I 158; P248 I 179; P271 I 193; P325 I 256; P365 I 289; P388 I 306; P392 I 308–309; P473 I 363; P493 I 375–376; P528 II 405; P615 II 473; P640 II 492–493; P709 II 544; P911 II 669; P922 II 674; P1138 III 800; P1414 III 981; Leyda II 475–476. For references to want and plenty, beggary and power, see P119 I 86; P355 I 283; P359 I 286; P377 I 299–300; P385 I 304–305; P406 I 316–317; P439 I 339; P490 I 373–374; P506 II 388–389; P523 II 401–402; P579 II 443; P690 II 533; P717 II 550; P726 II 555; P760 II 578–579; P763 II 580–581; P771 II 585; P773 II 586; P791 II 597; P801 II 606; P803 II 607; P815 II 616; P872 II 648–649; P1036 II 735; P1077 II 762; P1109 II 780–781; P1116 II 785; P1117 II 786; P1125 II 790; P1223 III 851–852; P1240 III 862; P1256 III 871; P1282 III 891; P1307 III 908; P1314 III 910; P1382 III 952; P1430 III 991; P1477 III 1022; P1567 III 1079; P1640 III 1123; P1675 III 1140–1141; P1772 III 1185; L III 859. For poems on mountains and daisies, see P124 I 89; P481 I 369; P666 II 512–513; P788 II 594–595; P975 II 705. For other daisy poems, see P85 I 69; P93 I 73–74; P102 I 78; P106 I 80; P337 I 269–270; P339 I 270–272; P411 I 320; P1037 III 735; P1232 III 857.

34. For poems on chivalry and fairy-tale, see P9 I 11–12; P32 I 29; P34 I 30–31; P53 I 40–41; P55 I 41; P64 I 49; P66 I 52; P117 I 85–86; P144 I 103–104; P235 I 170; P302 I 223; P336 I 269; P366 I 291–292; P373 I 296–297; P473 I 363; P506 II 388–389; P617 II 475;

P665 II 512; P865 II 646; P1224 III 852; P1305 III 907; P1353 III 934; P1361 III 940; P1620 III 1111.

35. For poems in which the poet is elevated by the King, see P73 I 58–59; P144 I 103–104; P166 I 121–122; P195 I 140; P217 I 155; P231 I 168; P247 I 177–178; P273 I 194–195; P323 I 253; P336 I 269; P343 I 274–275; P346 I 277; P373 I 296–297; P506 II 388–389; P631 II 485–486; P674 II 521; P721 II 552; P738 II 562–563; P803 II 607; P1001 II 723; P1011 II 726; P1072 II 758; P1079 II 763; P1426 III 989; P1567 III 1079; P1627 III 1116–1117; P1735 III 1167; P1737 III 1168–1169.

36. For wife poems, see P199 I 142–143; P461 I 355; P470 I 361–362; P493 I 375–376; P586 II 448; P732 II 558–559.

37. For bride poems, see P271 I 193; P283 I 202–203; P300 I 221–222; P473 I 363; P508 II 389–390; P631 II 485–486; P830 II 629; P1072 II 758; P1088 II 768; P1737 III 1168–1169.

38. Leyda II 76.

39. P580 II 444; P674 II 521; P679 II 525; L II 618; P124 I 89.

40. For poems in which the poet assumes a masculine role, see P683 II 529; P791 II 597; P980 II 708; P98 I 76; P199 I 142–143; P235 I 170; P356 I 283–284; P385 I 304–305; P430 I 333–334; P616 II 474; P642 II 494; P704 II 542.

41. L II 474, 478.

42. *Images or Shadows of Divine Things*, pp. 107–108, 123; see also Image no. 200, p. 130.

43. See Emerson's essay "Circles," in *Essays: First Series*. See also Emerson's poem "Uriel"; "The Uses of Great Men," *Representative Men*, pp. 36–37; and *Consciousness in Concord*, ed. Perry Miller (Boston, 1958), p. 201.

44. For references to expanding consciousness, see P378 I 300; P508 II 390; P533 II 409–410; P564 II 431; P646 II 497; P703 II 541; P760 II 578; P783 II 591; P798 II 604; P802 II 607; P967 II 699; P983 II 710; P1067 II 751; P1289 III 895; P1510 III 1042; P1541 III 1063; L I 264; L III 690, 720.

45. See *Nature*; Thoreau's "Walking," in *Excursions*; see also P680 II 526–527.

46. See Emerson's "Circles." P943 II 685; L II 430.

47. P1090 II 769; P1084 II 766; P1343 III 927–928.

48. For circumference as terminus, see P354 I 282–283; P552 II 422; P949 II 689. Emerson associates the two words at the end of the "Language" chapter of *Nature*.

49. P1695 III 1149; P865 II 646.

50. P889 II 656; P1428 III 990; P1663 III 1134.

51. P306 I 227; P1717 III 1158; P1428 III 990.

52. P802 II 607; P633 II 486.

53. For poems using "disk," see P909 II 668; P992 II 718; P1086 II 767; P1454 III 1006–1007; P1550 III 1069. For poems using "sheen," see P1315 III 910–911; P1450 III 1004; P1490 III 1029; P1584 III 1091–1092; P1550 III 1069.

54. In addition to the poems on awe cited in subsequent notes, see also P671 II 518–519; P683 II 529; P894 II 659; P1323 III 915; L II 517–518; L III 758, 817.

55. See P1609 III 1107; P210 I 148; L III 858; P1171 II 818; P974 II 704; P1173 II 819; L III 661; P1677 III 1141; P1678 III 1142; P1419 III 984–985; P1217 III 848; P1486 III 1027; P1677 III 1141; L II 507.

56. For awe as fear of danger or death, see P829 II 628; P1152 II 807; P1204 III 837; P1363 III 942; P1394 III 963; P1733 III 1166–1167; L II 423. For awe as privation, see P338 I 270; P564 II 431; P1171 II 818; P1370 III 946; L III 858. For awe as obscurity or mystery, see P1173 II 819; P1221 III 851; P1400 III 970–971. For awe as magnitude or infinity, see P564 II 431; P575 II 439; P963 II 697; P1353 III 934–935; L III 800. For awe as suddenness, see P974 II 704.

57. See Emerson's essay "The Oversoul," in *Essays: First Series*.

58. For poems on the partly known–partly unknown, see P210 I 148; P421 I 326–327; P1108 II 780; P1173 II 819; P1202 III 836; P1222 III 851; P1331 III 919; P1413 III 981; P1609 III 1107.

59. P1437 III 996; P1413 III 981; P1558 III 1072–1073.

CHAPTER VI: The Flower, the Bee, and the Spider

1. L II 404, 436.

2. P998 II 721.

3. See "The Natural History of Massachusetts," in *Excursions*.

4. P1775 III 1186; P1474 III 1020; P516 II 396.

5. P315 I 238. For the poet as seer, see also P155 I 111–112; P195 I 140; P306 I 227–228; P797 II 603.

6. P974 II 704; L II 474.

7. P785 II 592; P1472 III 1019.

8. For the adequacy of speech and silence, see P1048 II 740; P407 I 317. See also: P420 I 326; P581 II 444–445; P688 II 531; P797 II 603; P932 II 697; P989 II 715–716; P1126 II 790–791; P1225 III 853; P1358 III 939; P1668 III 1137; P1681 III 1143; P1750 III 1175; L II 336, 450; L III 878, 926. The quotation from Marianne Moore is from her poem "The Past Is the Present," *Collected Poems* (New York: Macmillan Co., 1951), p. 93.

9. P1251 III 868.

10. These quotations are taken from the *Paris Review* interview with Henry Miller, reprinted in *Writers at Work: Second Series* (New York, 1963), pp. 171–173.

11. See P81 I 66; P230 I 167; P1628 III 1117; P1772 III 1185; L II 532; L III 784–785.

12. From Thoreau's essay "Autumnal Hints," in *Excursions*.

13. P1628 III 1117; L II 455.

14. P505 II 388; P451 I 348; P601 II 461; L II 414; P1705 III 1153.

15. The poems referred to below in the text are: P96 I 75; P106 I 80; P65 I 50–51; P41 I 34; P91 I 73.

16. P31 I 29; P32 I 29.

17. P1058 II 746. See also P438 I 339; P1019 II 729; P1734 III 1167; L II 505.

18. From Thoreau's essay "Days and Nights in Concord," in *Excursions*.

19. P138 I 98; P916 II 671; P1337 III 924; P1339 III 925.

20. P319 I 243.

21. L II 554, 481; P1400 III 970.

22. P677 II 523; P448 I 347; P307 I 228; P308 I 229; P488 I 372–373; P681 II 528.

23. The quotations from Emerson throughout this passage are from "The Poet," in *Essays: Second Series*.

24. P1129 II 792; L III 858, 847, 850.

25. Leyda I 331; Thoreau, *Consciousness in Concord*, p. 179.

26. See P1467 III 1017; L II 612; L III 664, 858.

27. "A Conversation with Brother Antoninus," *The Harvard Advocate*, 97 (Spring 1963), 39.

28. L II 409.

29. For experiments with words, see, for example: "The Seldoms of the Mind" (L II 509); "Water grows," "That Caspian Fact," "Sahara dies" (P1291 III 896); "Zero at the Bone" (P986 II 712); "Summer's circumspect" (P1298 III 901); "Death's Immediately" (P1420 III 985); "Intro without my Trans" (P1530 III 1055); "Meek my Vive le roi" (P151 I 108); "Marine Walk" (L III 858); "a Must," "a Shall" (P1618 III 1110); "On their Passage Cashmere" (P86 I 70); "The Transitive of Bells" (P633 II 486–487); "among Circumference" (P798 II 604); "ablative to show" (P1744 III 1172). For coined words, see, for example: birdling (P39 I 33); swang (P42 I 35); o'ertakeless (P282 I 201); goer by (P283 I 202); New Englandly (P285 I 204); optizan (P329 I 263); crucifixal (P364 I 289); hostiler (P705 II 542); undivine (P751 II 572); consciouser (P762 II 580); vitalless (P770 II 584); perceiveless (P843 II 637); mis sum (P877 II 651); kinsmansless (P1019 II 729);

antiquest (P1068 II 752); exody (P1300 III 905); redoubtablest (P1417 III 983); graphicer (P1422 III 986); overtakelessness (P1691 III 1147).

30. Thoreau, *Consciousness in Concord*, p. 162.

31. P1275 III 886–887; P605 II 464.

CHAPTER VII: The Tightening Circle

1. *Images or Shadows of Divine Things*, pp. 3, 6.
2. *Ibid.*, p. 44.
3. In the "Language" chapter in *Nature*.
4. *Pierre*, bk. XXV, chap. iv.
5. From the "Preface" to *The Spoils of Poynton*.
6. *The Letters of Henry James* (London, 1920), pp. 506–508.
7. Certain kinds of abstraction in twentieth-century art can best be understood as the individual's attempt to work out a structure of relationships at least in the use of his materials. In words that closely parallel Stevens' premises, Stuart Davis has insisted that "the subject matter of painting includes the materials of expression." Consequently, "the act of painting is not a duplication of experience but an extension of experience on the plane of formal invention," and its end is the "objective order" of an "autonomous sensate object." In an extreme, almost mathematical, statement of the principle, a sculptor like José de Rivera makes the abstract design the only meaning: "The prime function is the total experience of the production. . . The content, beauty and source of excitement is inherent in the interdependence and relationship of the space, material and light, and is the structure." See E. C. Goossen, *Stuart Davis* (New York, 1959), pp. 13, 16, 17, 28; and John Gordon, *José de Rivera* (New York, 1961), p. 3.

This kind of formalist abstraction is diametrically opposed to the lyric impulse and free form of Jackson Pollack and most of the "action" painters and abstract expressionists. Their aim is not rigid control and deliberate pattern but, on the contrary, the unpredictable release of subconscious energies. In other words, Pollack tends to be Dionysian where Davis tends to be Apollonian.

8. See, for example, "How to Live. What to Do," "Credences of Summer," "This Solitude of Cataracts," "The Poem That Took the Place of a Mountain," and "The Poems of Our Climate."

9. Leyda I 201.

10. From Emerson's essay "The Transcendentalist," in *Nature, Addresses, and Lectures*.

11. See L III 727, 729; MacGregor Jenkins, *Emily Dickinson: Friend and Neighbor*, p. 65.

12. See, for example, L I 49; L II 324, 377, 416, 423, 436; L III 727, 739, 833, 849, 902, 924.

13. L I 245, 239, 150; L II 324, 483; Leyda II 474; L III 925.

14. L II 329. For references to insanity and madness, see P410 I 319; P435 I 337; P556 II 425; P576 II 440; P593 II 454–455; P617 II 475; P937 II 682; P1284 III 892; P1323 III 915; P1333 III 921; L I 182, 208; L II 329, 356, 376, 404, 424, 518–519, 526, 605; L III 754, 802–803.

15. P441 I 340; L II 460, L III 752.

16. L II 461.

17. L II 476.

18. P670 II 517; L II 412; Leyda II 478; L III 847; Leyda II 482, 481.

19. See Leyda II 125, 253, 483, 273, 116, 441, 120, 125, 115–116; Leyda I, xxix–xxx.

20. From the "Conclusion" of Pater's *Renaissance*.

21. Oscar Wilde, *De Profundis* (London, 1908), p. 15; *After Berneval: Letters of Oscar Wilde to Robert Ross* (Westminster, 1922), p. 21.

22. *The Notebooks and Papers of Gerard Manley Hopkins*, ed. Humphry House (London, 1937), p. 315.

23. L III 767. For references to foreign places in the poetry, see the following numbers (volume and page numbers are omitted to save space): 29, 59, 64, 73, 80, 86, 137, 138, 140, 179, 210, 214, 247, 252, 268, 276, 287, 295, 299, 300, 350, 373, 395, 403, 422, 430, 452, 453, 481, 492, 502, 506, 511, 513, 525, 531, 541, 553, 555, 574, 587, 597, 601, 602, 621, 628, 666, 697, 715, 716, 725, 746, 841, 862, 863, 872, 914, 970, 981, 991, 994, 1011, 1013, 1029, 1048, 1067, 1087, 1107, 1117, 1146, 1148, 1213, 1237, 1259, 1291, 1366, 1432, 1463, 1466, 1473, 1477, 1487, 1492, 1516, 1528, 1554, 1627, 1642, 1664, 1694, 1696, 1705, 1754. See also L II 453, 454, 455, 524, 551, 561, 585, 593, 605, 611, 637, 644, 645; L III 662, 666, 673, 691, 709, 710, 724, 728, 765, 783, 791, 811, 823, 833, 834.

24. Thoreau, *Journals*, I, 247–248.

25. L II 350; Emerson's essay on "Thoreau," in *Lectures and Biographical Sketches*.

26. L II 576.

27. P680 II 526–527.

28. L I 209–210.

29. L II 412. See "The Transcendentalist," in *Nature, Addresses, and Lectures*.

INDEX

INDEX